Jesus

and

Politics

Zacchaeus Studies: New Testament

General Editor: Mary Ann Getty

Jesus

and

Politics

by

Seán P. Kealy C.S.Sp.

A Michael Glazier Book
THE LITURGICAL PRESS
Collegeville, Minnesota

About the Author

Seán P. Kealy, C.S.Sp., is President of Blackrock College in Dublin. He is a former Rector of Holy Ghost Missionary College, also in Dublin. Fr. Kealy served as a missionary for many years in Kenya, where he was a professor of scripture at Kenyatta University. Among his publications is *The Apocalypse of John.*

A Michael Glazier Book
published by
THE LITURGICAL PRESS

Cover design by Maureen Daney. Typography by Phyllis Boyd LeVane.

1   2   3   4   5   6   7   8   9

Library of Congress Cataloging-in-Publication Data

Kealy, Seán P.
   Jesus and politics / by Seán P. Kealy.
       p.   cm. — (Zacchaeus studies.   New Testament.)
   "A Michael Glazier book."
   Includes bibliographical references and index.
   ISBN 0-8146-5668-4 (pbk.)
   1. Jesus Christ—Political and social views.   2. Bible.   N.T.
Gospels—Criticism, interpretation, etc.   3. Zealots (Jewish party)
4. Palestine—History—To 70 A.D.   I. Title.   II. Series.
BS2417.P6K4   1990
232—dc19   88-82450
                                                                              CIP

Contents

There is a time for everything, and many a man desires a reformation of an abuse, or the fuller development of a doctrine, or the adoption of a particular policy, but forgets to ask himself whether the right time for it is come: and, knowing that there is no one who will be doing anything towards its accomplishment in his own life-time unless he does it himself, he will not listen to the voice of authority, and he spoils a good work in his own century, in order that another man, as yet unborn, may not have the opportunity of bringing it happily to perfection in the next. He may seem to the world to be nothing else than a bold champion for the truth and a martyr to free opinion, when he is just one of those persons whom the competent authority ought to silence.

John Henry Newman, *Apologia Pro Vita Sua.* *

* London: Collins Fontana, 1972, pp. 291-292.

Editor's Note

Zacchaeus Studies provide concise, readable and relatively inexpensive scholarly studies on particular aspects of scripture and theology. The New Testament section of the series presents studies dealing with focal or debated questions; and the volumes focus on specific texts of particular themes of current interest in biblical interpretation. Specialists have their professional journals and other forums where they discuss matters of mutual concern, exchange ideas and further contemporary trends of research; and some of their work on contemporary biblical research is now made accessible for students and others in *Zacchaeus Studies*.

The authors in this series share their own scholarship in non-technical language, in the areas of their expertise and interest. These writers stand with the best in current biblical scholarship in the English-speaking world. Since most of them are teachers, they are accustomed to presenting difficult material in comprehensible form without compromising a high level of critical judgment and analysis.

The works of this series are ecumenical in content and purpose and cross credal boundaries. They are designed to augment formal and informal biblical study and discussion. Hopefully they will also serve as texts to enhance and supplement seminary, university and college classes. The series will also aid Bible study groups, adult education and parish religious education classes to develop intelligent, versatile and challenging programs for those they serve.

Mary Ann Getty
New Testament Editor

Preface

Africa is a wonderful place to learn about God, people and politics. I was very fortunate to have spent many years there when so many new nations with much flag-waving and hand-clapping had just entered upon independence. Robert Ruark, with rather uncomplimentary and patronizing bluntness, in the foreword to his novel, *Uhuru,* vividly portrayed some of the expectations:

> The title of this book is *Uhuru,* the one word most frequently heard in East Africa these days. It means, roughly, 'freedom' and is used and abused according to personal inclination.
>
> Uhuru is a Semitic word used commonly in both Arabic and Hebraic, and it sneaked into Swahili, which is the lingua franca of East and Central Africa, via the slave trade. Uhuru is synonymous to 'l'independence' in the Congo, or 'free-dom' in West Africa. It has become in recent months so much part of daily use that it is employed by black and white alike, in much the same sense that 'liberté, fraternité, égalité' were adopted in the French Revolution.
>
> One can rarely pick up a newspaper in East Africa today without seeing Uhuru glaring a dozen times. One cannot stride a street or ride the roads of even back-country Kenya without being greeted by the old Churchillian 'V' sign, or a Nazi-esque flattened palm accompanied by a ringing shout

of Uhuru. One cannot eavesdrop a conversation amongst white or black or rich or poor station without hearing the word repeated over and over again.

Each native African has his own concept of 'Uhuru.' For some it is a mythical description of a round-the-corner Utopia of slothful ease, of plentiful booze and an altogether delightfully dreamy state in which money grows on bushes and all human problems are ended. To the nomadic grazier it means endless flocks of lovely useless cattle and gorgeous land-ruining goats—with infinite vistas of lush pasturage, and water galore between two suns' march. To the ivory poacher, it is an absence of game wardens and stuffy restrictive game laws. To the meat-eater, it is limitless meat and plenitude of free salt; to the drunkard, a sea of honey beer; to the womanizer, a harem which stretches to the horizon. To the peasant African farmer, it is the white man's magically rich and loamy land which will certainly be his on the magic day of 'Uhuru,' when the white man is driven from the continent and all the carefully nurtured soil reverts to the African. To the wilfully lawless, 'Uhuru' is a license to rob and steal, to kill without punishment and to flout rules of decent human behaviour with reckless impunity.

'Uhuru' to the white man takes on a slightly different complexion. 'Uhuru' is regarded as a threat—a threat to his white property, a threat to his white women, a threat to his white life of toil and his momentary white life of ease with plenty of black boys to hurry at his bidding and to murmur respectful 'Yes, Bwana' to his every command, no matter how illogical. 'Uhuru' is a threat to his concept of himself as a white master of a suppressed black race, and represents a sudden violent rearrangement of himself in the old Poona '02 concept of 'Bwana Mkubwa' or 'great White Lord.'

But I was privileged to share in listening, teaching and lecturing with many who were struggling to understand what the Christian notion of freedom really involved. Coming from a country where the 'Fight for Irish Freedom' was so idealized, it was a fascinating experience to question one's own emotions and dreams, to sympathise with the widespread failure to build solid and lasting political structures in Africa and to suffer as one watched conditions become much harsher in some ways than under the Empire, with massive national debts, interior division and inefficient and incompetent administrations. Looking back over some of my lecture notes from those days I found such idealistic reflections on freedom as the following:

"The Christian notion of freedom or Uhuru for a people means the well-being of all sections of the population, ranging from soundness of body to that full real living whose quality can best be described in the Biblical term of 'eternal life.' Christ came to take away the sin of the world, to set people free that they may have life and have it abundantly. This means a *freedom from* all kinds of evil and error, from sickness to polytheism, but above all a *freedom to* a new kind of life in which loving acceptance of God is central and we are enabled to live out in the concrete situation the will of God, with all our hearts. This Uhuru is described under many names in the Bible from peace to salvation to happiness. But this Uhuru, the Christian holds, no politician or revolution can give or achieve. However, it is often promised and expected and this history shows that the setting up of independent political countries has often brought disappointment and disillusionment. Too much is expected from political change or revolution. Too often the achievement of political independence is seen as the solution to all problems of all segments of the population. This, of course, as history clearly bears witness, has never happened and never will happen. Politics, we are told, is the art of the possible, the humanly possible, the compromise. Christianity is the 'impossible dream,' the art of the humanly impossible. A Christian is not guided by the expedient or by cautious calculation of safe consequences, but by awareness of the voice and will of God. To the Christian there are no mountains. This is not to condemn the politician or the revolutionary, but to indicate how easily conflict can occur."

Harvey Cox's book, *The Secular City,* with its emphasis on the Exodus as the model confrontation between Church and State, was important:

In tracing the desacralization of politics to its biblical roots, the Exodus must be the focal point of study. For the Hebrews Yahweh had spoken decisively not in a natural phenomenon, such as a thunderclap or an earthquake, but through a historical event, the deliverance from Egypt. It is particularly significant that this was an event of social change, a massive act of what we might today call 'civil disobedience.' It was an act of insurrection against a duly constituted monarch, a Pharaoh whose relationship to the sun-god reconstituted his claim to political sovereignity. There had no doubt been similar escapes before, but the Exodus of the Hebrews became more than a minor event which happened to an unimportant people. It became the central event around which the Hebrews organised their whole perception of reality. As such, it symbolized the deliverance of man out of a sacral-political order and into history and social change, where political leadership would be based on power gained by the capacity to accomplish specific social objectives.

The Exodus delivered the Jews from Egypt, yet there was a persistent temptation to return to sacral politics, especially during the period of the monarchy. But the prophetic bands always stood in the way, preventing such a relapse. Since the prophets always had a source of authority separate from the royal favour, the priest-king was never really possible again. The Exodus had made it forever impossible to accept without reservation the sanctions of any monarch. Yahweh could always stage a new Exodus, or work through history to bring down a monarch with delusions of grandeur. No royal house was ever afterwards unquestionably secure on its throne.

Important too was the agreement at the August 1969 consultation of the World Council of Churches:

All else failing, the Church and Churches support resistance movements, including revolutions which aim at the elimination of political or economic tyranny which makes racism possible.

But the contemporary model was Martin Luther King who though of a rich and comfortable background became involved with the rights of his poorer brothers and proposed the following ten commandments as a blueprint for the Christian revolutionary of our day:

1. MEDITATE daily on the teachings and life of Jesus.
2. REMEMBER always that the non-violent movement...seeks justice and reconciliation, not victory.
3. WALK and TALK in the manner of love, for God is love.
4. PRAY daily to be used by God in order that all men may be free.
5. SACRIFICE personal wishes in order that all men may be free.
6. OBSERVE with both friend and foe the ordinary rules of courtesy.
7. SEEK to perform regular service for others and for the world.
8. REFRAIN from violence of fist, tongue or heart.
9. STRIVE to be in good spiritual and bodily health.
10. FOLLOW the directions of the movement and the captain of the demonstration.

However, I was gradually forced to read more widely and to examine the biblical evidence for myself. The following pages then are the fruit. They are dedicated with much respect to Catholic and Protestant missionaries of East Africa. Miss Gemma McKenna kindly helped with the typing. Fr. A. Flood C.S.Sp. provided the detailed indices. But it was Sister Tina Heeran, M.S.H.R. who with her incredible generosity typed and retyped an unreadable manuscript.

Seán P. Kealy C.S.Sp.
The Feast of Pentecost

Introduction

Politics, according to Edmund Burke, should not be heard in the pulpit. For the only voice which should be heard there, is the healing voice of Christian love. Would that the problem had that simple a solution! The question of the politics of Jesus and the resulting tension between politics and religion is one that simply will not go away. No Church can completely escape a political dimension to its activities and its influence although few Churches in history have made politics a primary concern. Even Dietrich Bonhoeffer, whom many consider to be one of the saints of the twentieth century, was involved in a plot to overthrow Hitler by violence. Like Hydras' heads, the problem continually surfaces in the most unlikely places, such as the late Dean Inge who reminded his wealthy West End congregation some fifty years ago that the Magnificat was a much more revolutionary anthem than the communist Internationale, or George Bernard Shaw's preface to *Androcles and the Lion:*

> The iconolaters have never for a moment conceived Jesus as a real person, who meant what he said, as a fact, as a force like electricity, only needing the invention of suitable political machinery to be applied to the affairs of mankind with revolutionary effect. Thus it is not disbelief that is dangerous to our society; it is belief. The moment it strikes you (as it may any day) that Jesus is not the lifeless, harmless image

he has hitherto been to you, but a rallying centre for revolutionary influence, which all established States and Churches fight, you must look to yourselves, for you have brought the image to life, and the mob may not be able to stand that horror.

or the Jamaican folksinger Bob Marley:

Me don' understand politics, me don' understand big words like "democratic socialism." What me say is what de Bible say, but because people don' read de Bible no more, dey tink me talk politics. Ha! It's de Bible what have it written and it strong, it powerful.[1]

Robert McAfee Brown shows us that reading the Bible through Third World eyes reveals unsuspected aspects and especially how in the West we have often domesticated the cutting edge of the biblical message. He quotes how the Sri Lankan priest, Tissa Balasuriya, has reminded us in *The Eucharist and Human Liberation* that

the central act of Christian Liberation is the celebration of a political act of liberation by God, and that every repetition of the Eucharist should signify a new commitment to the struggle for justice. Fr. Balasuriya chides us for having tamed the Eucharist, distorting its revolutionary implications into a time for reaffirming the status quo. But he takes heart from the fact that as the true roots of the original event are being rediscovered in the third world, the dynamic for change is returning. True celebration of the Eucharist is an act of revolutionary politics. Any smart dictator will forbid it on pain of death.[2]

[1] Robert McAfee Brown, *Unexpected News* (Philadelphia: Westminster Press, 1984).

[2] Ibid., p. 124.

Many other examples can be given such as Ernst Käsemann, who wrote his commentary of Hebrews[3] while under arrest in 1937. He was put in jail for criticizing the Nazi regime. There, disgusted with the popular servility to Hitler, he discovered in Hebrews a powerful antidote. No earthly city can replace the heavenly Jerusalem. Christ alone is Lord and Leader of the people, who must live as struggling pilgrims walking by faith towards an unseen goal.

The political question has become a very crucial one in modern times as is evident from the popular book, *Unyoung, Uncoloured and Unpoor*.[4] Morris, a Methodist minister in Zambia and adviser to President Kaunda, had arrived in Zambia carrying beneath his arm Trevor Huddleston's *Naught for Your Comfort*,[5] a book described as the greatest to come out of the African church in the 1950s. *Naught for Your Comfort* was a "searing condemnation in the unmitigated light of the love of God for the structural inhumanity of South African society and apartheid policy as seen in the slums of Johannesburg."[6] Morris' own book was written out of his deep personal experience of the problems of the Third World. It was a passionately sincere attempt to find out how Jesus himself would react to such a situation. The theme of his book is bluntly summarised on its back cover

> that the world is ruled by the Unyoung, Uncoloured and Unpoor and that only violent revolution will overthrow

[3]Ernst Käsemann, *Das wandernde Gottesvolk: Eine Untersuching zum Hebraerbrief*, 4 Aufl. (Göttingen: Vandenhoeck & Ruprecht, 1961); English trans., *The Wandering People of God: An Investigation of the Letter to the Hebrews*, trans. Roy A. Harrisville and Irving L. Sandburg (Minneapolis: Ausgburg Publishing House, 1984).

[4]Colin Morris, *Unyoung, Uncolored, Unpoor* (Nashville: Abingdon, 1969).

[5]London: Collins, 1965.

[6]Adrian Hastings, *A History of African Christianity (1950-1975)*. (Cambridge: University Press, 1979), p. 104. Morris was also influenced by the writings of S.G.F. Brandon; cf. below, note 52.

them in order to give the majority of the world's population their due place in the sun. Claiming that the Christian has both the right and the responsibility to take part in this struggle, Morris offers a re-interpretation of Jesus which challenges the traditional view that he was innocent of sedition against the Roman authorities.

Certainly, Jesus lived in a very turbulent period in Jewish history, the seething cauldron of first century Palestine, as a recent author describes it.[7] Yet the period of his public ministry was not the most outstanding for its violence towards the Roman occupation. The fact is that Josephus, the Jewish historian, describes no conspiracies between 6-44 A.D. However, the problem with Jesus is that he is everybody's Rorschach test. People tend to see in him what their psyche's crave. It is almost impossible to examine him objectively. The way one reacts has a lot to do with one's hidden agenda, with one's political stance in the modern world, activist, comfortable, conservative or otherwise. Nevertheless, any conclusion as to Jesus' political involvement is quite compatible with an orthodox belief in his divinity. The problem lies in the consequences for Christian morality and political activity.

The traditional Christian view as exemplified by most missionaries in the 1950s was to a large extent apolitical.[8] Religion

---

[7]J. Massyngbaerde Ford, *My Enemy is My Guest* (New York: Orbis, 1984), pp. 1-2.

[8]According to J.B. Metz (*Theology of the World.* [London: Herder & Herder, 1969], p. 109), Christian theology both Protestant and Catholic before the 1960s operated with the categories of the intimate, the private, the apolitical sphere. Gabriel Daly in *Irish Challenges to Theology,* ([Dublin: Dominican Publications, 1986], p. 88), quotes David Jenkin's blunt critique of Churches which, in an attempt to "keep their hands clean" try to neglect the political dimension and concentrate only on what they call "spiritual" things. He accuses them of both deceiving themselves and failing in their public duty: "Christians cannot escape from the problems inherent in living in this world by creating for themselves some kind of ecclesiastical buffer-state whose symbols and procedures claim a unique purity because they refer only to ecclesiastical affairs."

and politics were quite different things and the Church's mission was about the former. The really important matters were spiritual, not political. Jesus' own messiahship was non-political and his kingdom was not of this world. Like Paul (Romans 13) they accepted the existing political powers as temporary and as tolerated if not directly willed by God. They tended to distrust the rise of movements towards self-government and at best hoped that independence would not happen too soon.[9] But the Solomonic distinction between religion and politics has never been a satisfactory one.[10]

In the struggle between Church and State which assumed such dramatic and even heroic forms in certain European countries during the rise and fall of Hitlerism, a great revival of biblical study began to sweep the world, affecting both Catholic, Orthodox and Protestant. In the name of the supreme lordship of Jesus, whose universal sway over earth as well as heaven is part of the central teaching of the Bible, many Christians, hitherto rather indifferent to social problems, experienced radical conversions.[11] Oscar Romero, the murdered Archbishop of San Salvador could write:

[9]Historically the Church's moral teaching has put its main emphasis on the individual's duties. The morality of society has been less emphasized while the international domain has received even less stress. Fortunately in recent years there has been some corrective emphasis in these areas.

[10]A reading of the OT, especially the legal sections of Leviticus and Deuteronomy, shows that the Jewish people did not distinguish between religious and secular, between civil and personal law and ethics or even between moral and ceremonial norms. All were geared towards living life to the full in a covenant relationship between God and the whole people and embraced every area of life.

[11]Few, however, would go as far as the statement attributed to Imam Khomeini of Iran. "Our politics is religion and our religion is our politics." In Germany Goebbels said: "Churchmen dabbling in politics should take note that their only task is to prepare for the world hereafter." To Niemoller who said that he was concerned for the future of the German nation, Hitler is said to have replied: "Let that be my concern."

> It is practically illegal to be an authentic Christian in our environment...precisely because the world which surrounds us is founded on an established disorder before which the mere proclamation of the Gospel is subversive.[12]

Pope Paul VI's *Populorum Progressio* was considered by a number of Latin American governments to be too radical to be disseminated because of such statements as

> The earth's goods must be divided fairly and this right of everyone to a just share comes first. Even the right of private property, and the right to free enterprise, must yield to justice.

Today, then, it seems clearer than ever, that there is no real choice between political involvement and non-involvement for the Church. All questions are ultimately religious and in need of theological reflection in a never-ending circle. Or as Péguy once put it "Everything begins in mysticism and ends in politics." For even to remain silent in the face of practices or situations which are antithetical to the all-embracing kingdom is to take a political stance of tacit permission and to risk being unfaithful to the mission of Jesus and the Church. The dilemma is how to speak on issues while avoiding the accusation of meddling in politics. Not surprisingly, left-wing Christians are enthusiastic about the discovery of an explicitly left-wing Jesus. On the other hand right-wing Christians find such a portrayal as virtually blasphemous. All agree that the dominant model for the Christian is that of the mission and actual experience of Jesus himself in the world. Today it is becoming increasingly accepted that Jesus was far more politically minded and far more concerned with the political life of his nation in relation to God's all-embracing purposes than many pious Christians have often supposed. According to A.M. Hunter:[13]

[12] *Tablet,* 24/31 December 1983, p. 1251.

[13] *The Parables Then and Now,* (London, S.C.M., 1971), pp. 90f.

One of the many gospel evidences in proof of this is the parable of the Way to Court, or, as it is often called, the Defendant. It concludes a passage (Lk 12:35-39) heavy with Jesus' foreboding about the crisis which overhung Israel. Read it again, and you will see that the parable is the last of five (the others are the Waiting Servants, the Sleeping Householder, the Man in Charge, and the Weather Signs) in which Jesus foresees the coming crisis and calls on his country-men to read the signs of the times and act accordingly. 'How weather-wise you can all be' he says to them, 'O if only you could be as spiritually wide-awake to what is happening in this nation now!' Then he speaks the parable of the Way to Court. . . .There are four parties in the parable—the insolent debtor, the creditor, the judge and the constable. How do we interpret it? The insolent debtor on the way to court is Israel. The way to court is Jesus' way of describing the impending crisis in his nation's history, a crisis which, he says, will bring testing for his followers, God's judgement on the nation and a blood baptism for himself. Israel stands at the crossroads, and she must decide which way she will go. She must choose whether to align herself with God's purpose embodied in himself and his ministry, or refusing and pursuing the path of nationalism, enter on a collision course with Rome which must end in her ruin.

What makes the decision so urgent is the shortness of the time. If his countrymen were in similar straits financially, if they were insolent debtors on the way to court, they would settle with their creditor long before they reached it. But alas, in the far more momentous crisis of their nation, "eyes have they but they see not." Could they but realize their peril, they would see that the only right thing to do was to turn, before it was too late., and come penitently to the living God whose great purpose in history goes forward whether men will or not!

Consider the historical situation as Jesus saw it in the light of God's purpose for the world. God has chosen Israel to be his servant—to be the bearer to the world of a 'light to enlighten the Gentiles' that they too might come to a knowledge of his saving truth. But Israel, by rejecting God's kingdom and Messiah, was repudiating her part in God's great plan.

Thus it has gradually dawned in recent years that there is not only a considerable amount in the New Testament concerning the political responsibility and activity of a Christian but even far more than many were prepared to expect. C.E.B. Cranfield[14] has roughly indicated the various ranges of material which should be taken into account in three sections as follows. However, he rightly insists that passages in the first section will be certainly misinterpreted if they are interpreted in isolation from passages in the other two sections.[15]

1) Passages which contain direct exhortation on the subject: Mk 12:13-17 (Mt 22:15-22; Lk 20:20-26); Rom 13:1-7; 1 Tim 2:1-7; Tit 3:1-2; 1 Pet 2:13-17.

2) Passages which have some sort of reference to the state:

a) Passages which throw light on Jesus' attitude to the state: Mk 10:42 (Mt 20:25; Lk 22:25) on the lording attitude of the Gentile rulers over their subjects; Lk 13:32 on "that fox" Herod; Mk 13:9 (Mt 10:18; Lk 21:12-13) on standing before governors and kings for Christ's sake.

---

[14]C.E.B. Cranfield, *The Bible and Christian Life,* (Edinburgh, T & T Clark, 1985), p. 48. In an interesting article entitled "The Bible as a Political Document," (in *Explorations in Theology,* vol. 7), James Barr distinguishes six political images to be found in the Bible: theocratic, neutral, prophetic, the migrating nation, the new world and liberation.

[15]One can, for example, misinterpret the OT prohibition against stealing in such an individualistic ethic, which will not disturb the status quo, that one avoids the cutting edge of the biblical ethic. However, in the Bible this prohibition must be seen as part of a whole ethical vision. In this vision people came before property and the test of the development of society is the concern for the poor, the defenseless and the stranger. This vision was particularly emphasised in the Jubilee legislation according to which loans should be interest free, generous, wages should be paid on time, debts cancelled in the seventh year, and slaves set free, with the poor having a right to what grew in the fields lying fallow.

b) The Passion narratives.

c) The Birth narratives.

d) Paul's attitude to the state: 1 Cor 2:6-8 the rulers of this world are ignorant of the divine wisdom which he teaches; 1 Cor 6:1-6 the warning against taking a dispute with a fellow Christian before a heathen court; Acts 16:19-39 Paul's imprisonment at Philippi and his insistence that the magistrates should come in person to release him; the last chapters of Acts, from 21:31 onwards.

e) Revelation 13 (the passage about the beast from the abyss).

3) Passages which, while not referring to, yet have an important bearing upon the state and the Christian's political responsibility.

a) Passages which deal with the rule of the exalted Christ.

b) Passages concerned with eschatology.

c) Passages which make clear the reality and universality of sin.

d) Passages which reveal to us in our fellow person "the brother for whose sake Christ died."

e) Passages containing ethical teaching, especially those concerned with love to one's neighbour; and perhaps we should add—

f) Passages concerning the law.

1

Five Main Political Options
at the Time of Jesus

Any adequate portrayal of Jesus must attempt to answer
such questions as why Jesus attracted such attention, why he
was killed, how it was that a Jesus who lived completely
within Judaism was the origin of a movement which formed a
persecuted messianic sect which separated from Judaism and
why he was subsequently deified.[16]

A basic assumption of this study is that the standard options
and tendencies of the human condition in Jesus' day were not
radically different from that of our own.[17] The names might be
different but the Pharisees, Sadducees, Essenes, Zealots, Bap-

---

[16]In *Jesus and Judaism,* (London: SCM, 1985; Philadelphia: Fortress
Press, 1985), E.P. Sanders gives an excellent statement of the problems
involved. He draws on the work of Joseph Klausner, the first Jew who dared
to write a life of Jesus. *Jesus of Nazareth. His Life, Times, and Teaching*
(Jerusalem, 1922; trans. Herbert Danby [London/New York: The Macmillan
Company, 1925]). Klausner concluded his study with the statement that "to
adopt the teaching of Jesus is to remove oneself from the whole sphere of
ordered national and human existence" (E.T., 206).

[17]In *Galilee from Alexander the Great to Hadrian 323 BCE to 135 BCE.
A Study of Second Temple Judaism* ([Notre Dame: University Press/Wil-
mington, Delaware: Michael Glazier, Inc. 1980], pp. 208-255), Sean Freyne
argues that the revolutionary atmosphere in Galilee has been greatly exaggerated. This lends credence to the view that Jesus aimed at restoration in
Judaism without the use of armed force.

tists, Scribes, Samaritans, Herodians, tax-collectors, the pious few, the agnostics and practical atheists, the mass who live "lives of quiet desperation," are all still with us. From a careful study of these movements, their differing ways of life, their interpretation of the Bible, views on God, expectations and beliefs such as those concerning the after-life, the resurrection and angels, prayer and fasting, one can have a clearer understanding of the compassionate mission of Jesus and the options which he deliberately chose.[18] Jesus' world was far from monolithic. There was no clearcut orthodoxy to which all had to subscribe. His world consisted in an almost unlimited variety of attempts to define what Judaism was and should become. At least five main options were open to the Jews in the complicated political world of Jesus' day.[19] Jesus was well aware of the leaven of the Herods, the Pilates, the rich, the powerful churchmen, the popular terrorists. He made it painfully clear

[18]See my *Who is Jesus of Nazareth?* (Denville, N.M.: Dimension Books, 1978) *The Mission of Jesus* (Dublin: Dominican Publications, 1989) for a fuller elaboration of the problems involved.

[19]Society was basically divided into three classes: (a) the numerically small but wealthy and powerful ruling class in the Roman administration, the royal court of the Herodians and high priestly families; (b) the lower class which included the ordinary villagers and the large majority of agricultural peasants, the ordinary priests and temple officials and the workers in the cities; (c) the slaves with no rights. Thus there was nothing like our middle class. However, according to Richard A. Horsley, ("'Like One of the Prophets of Old': Two Types of Popular Prophets at the Time of Jesus," *CBQ* 47 [1985], 435- 468), there was in Palestinian Jewish society "at least a tiny but distinctive middle stratum of the literate group called 'philosophies' or 'parties' by Josephus (and often 'sects' by modern scholars), i.e. the Essenes who withdrew from the rest of society, the Pharisees who remained socially-politically engaged, and, for a time, the more activist 'Fourth Philosophy.' One problem was the diversity of material in the Jewish tradition which could be used to support different political options. In support of political revolution one could use the stories in which Elisha initiated coups d'etat against both Israel and Syria (2 Kgs 8:13; 9:1-3). On the other hand the action of David can be taken to mean that a political revolution is against the will of God. Because he was God's anointed, David spared Saul when he was in his power and further he dealt harshly with those who claimed to have killed Saul and his son" (1 Sam 26:8f; 2 Sam 1:14 -16; 4:9-12). (p. 444)

that none of these were to be models for his disciples when he described the truly blessed.[20]

1) Opportunistic Herodians

There was the way of the opportunistic Herodian princes and their sycophantic followers, who, though not full-blooded Jews, with Roman connivance had become the heirs to the achievements of the Maccabean dynasty. Jesus was born during the reign of Herod the Great when Augustus was Roman Emperor. He lived most of his life in Galilee under Herod Antipas and died in Jerusalem when Tiberius was Emperor. Herod Antipas, who ruled over Galilee and Peraea, outlived Jesus until his exile to Lyons in 39 A.D. Jesus was aware that John the Baptist had criticized Antipas for marrying his brother's wife and "for all the evil things Herod had done" (Lk 3:19). According to Luke (13:1) Jesus had received a report about some fellow Galileans "whose blood Pilate had mixed with their sacrifices" and soon afterwards he tells how Jesus

[20]Admittedly the gospel portraits and the writing of many theologians tend somewhat of necessity towards caricature in their portrayal of the movements in Jesus' day. Caricatures tend to distort the picture in a given direction and do not try to give the whole objective picture. Nevertheless, they are valuable in emphasizing salient features which tend to be distorted in a more objective presentation. The following quotation given by Sanders in *Jesus and Judaism* (p. 360) provides a badly needed corrective from the historical point of view: "In some presentations, 'Jesus increases in stature and wisdom and in favor with God and man' in direct proportion to the extent to which his contemporaries decrease—that is, they are invariably portrayed as narrow-minded legalists (Pharisees), fanatical nationalists (Zealots), sophisticated skeptics (Sadducees), esoteric sectarians (Essenes), and persons devoid of religious sensitivities altogether ('am-ha-arez'). When Jesus is played off against such a milieu, his appeal is purchased too cheaply. The error of the old liberal lives of Jesus lay precisely here—they lionized Jesus by playing him off against both Christian theology and the Judaism of which he was a part in order to present an appealing hero of liberal religion and ethics. As we saw in the previous chapter the same error is made by Fuchs and Bornkamm: Jesus 'brings God to speech in a culture existentially devoid of God.'"

received a warning from certain Pharisees—"Leave this place! Herod is trying to kill you" (13:31). Jesus, in one of his sharpest and rather scornful rebukes, and a rare political remark at that, insists that he will not alter his course and that the hen (v 34) is not intimidated by the fox (perhaps this word should be translated by 'jackal'). In Jewish literature a fox was considered to be a destructive animal and rather second rate in comparison with a lion (Ezek 13:4). In Luke 22:24ff Jesus criticizes Gentile kings for dominating their people and warns his disciples that they will be brought before such people (Lk 21:12-15). Herod is mentioned in six passages in Luke (one in Matthew and two in Mark) and figures in each major section of his gospel (3:1, 19; 8:31; 9:7-9; 13:31-35; 23:6-12). In the last passages Jesus is sent by Pilate to the Galilean Herod who obviously has some jurisdiction over him. Jesus' silent refusal to co-operate with Herod is highly significant and has been called his sharpest rebuke in the gospels (Is 53:17). Herod typifies the insincere politician, the superficial questioner who is not really interested in understanding Jesus' claims, his values or his political way of life.

2) Rich Aristocratic Sadducees

A second political option was to follow the rich aristocratic Sadducees and their way of political compromise with the Romans.[21] In theory at least for the Jewish people, there should

[21]Ellis Rivkin, *What Crucified Jesus? The Political Execution of a Charismatic,* (Nashville: Abingdon, 1984), gives a good exposé of the political scene in Palestine and concludes that the gospel portrayal of the death of Jesus makes sense. It was an execution arranged by the High Priest and his privy council, the Sanhedrin. For them Jesus' obvious lack of military ambition would have been of little or no concern at all. Religious claims to autonomy and Roman claims to sovereignty were almost impossible to separate. For Rivkin the situation was one of seething discontent and the authorities were fearful of any charismatic incitement. Jesus' action in the temple lent force to the political charge. It was the Roman imperial system which caused Jesus' death and not the system of Judaism with its differing

be no separation between Church and State. However, in the post-exilic period especially with the coming of the Romans and their puppet rulers, such a separation was enforced. Nevertheless, the Sadducees would have seen themselves as the rulers of Judaism in both religious and political affairs. They attempted to control society in collaboration with the Romans and would logically be concerned to suppress trouble makers like Jesus or such leaders of the people who would regularly spring up in such situations. These had achieved power and wealth in society in addition to controlling the temple, the symbolic centre of Judaism.

The Sadducean party was composed of a majority of the leading priests and the wealthy laity. According to Josephus[22] the Sadducees had the confidence of the wealthy alone and no following among the people. Once Jesus enters Jerusalem the Pharisees almost vanish from the scene and the Sadducees emerge as his adversaries. However, being leaders of Judaism, his activities hitherto could hardly have escaped their notice in such a small country. Jesus' lifestyle and values were quite opposed to theirs. The Good Samaritan parable with its comparison between the neglect of the temple officials and the compassion of the outcast Samaritan would not have endeared Jesus to the Jewish authorities. Jesus' cleansing of the temple with its overtones of a similar action by Judas Maccabaeus was a blunt challenge to their authority as the subsequent controversy shows (Lk 20:2). Further, the gospels show Jesus as describing the temple in a phrase from Jeremiah as a "den of robbers" (Lk 19:46). He bluntly criticizes the chief priests as selfish and even murderous tenants (Lk 20:9-16).

However, in describing Jesus as a critic of official Judaism one must be careful of portraying Jesus as embodying the true Old Testament spirit while describing Judaism as a merely

theologies and party conflicts. Rivkin, who obviously sympathizes with the Pharisees, points out that the special rules of the Pharisees only governed Pharisees. They did not bring the Sadducees or any other group to court for contravening their own rules.

[22] *Antiq.* 13:10.6.

priestly and legalistic distortion. Not all priests were so. Judaism in the time of Jesus has been re-evaluated by E.P. Sanders[23] as much more a religion of love, joy and grace than has hitherto been popular among scholars. For Sanders, Jesus was not executed because of theological disagreements about grace, forgiveness or merit, or because of such minor points of observance as handwashing or eating grain on the Sabbath. He sees some recent scholars turning away from theological fantasy towards historical realism. The setting for Jesus' death was one of seething discontent and fear of charismatic incitement while the cause was a political charge made particularly significant by Jesus' action in the temple.

It should be noted that

> the priests, not the prophets, were the real custodians of the care of souls in ancient Israel and priestly theology created a universe of meaning which would deal with the totality of life in its many dimensions and exigencies. There was certainly nothing less spiritual about cultic and legal piety than about prophetic proclamation; in fact, probably the opposite was the case.[24]

3) Essenes

A third political option was that of the Essenes. Disgusted with the corrupt officials of the Temple and pessimistic about the radical sinfulness of human nature,[25] their approach, in sharp contrast to that of Jesus and the Pharisees, was to withdraw from Temple worship and from society in general. The Essenes, who considered the Pharisees as too smooth in their biblical interpretation, were probably also descended from the Hasidim or pious people who had returned from Babylon.

[23]In *Jesus and Judaism,*

[24]John H. Hayes and Frederick C. Prussner, *Old Testament Theology* (London: SCM, 1985), p. 276.

[25]IQH 16:11; 1QS 11; CD1.

Under the leadership of the "one who teaches rightly" they were disillusioned with the Jewish leadership, their temple ritual and policies. Their hatred of the "Wicked Priest" and the "Spouter of lies" and the "breakers of the covenant" is very evident in their extant commentary on Habakkuk. However, this hard line is not consistently found in all their writings.[26]

Like the Pharisees they were not strictly pacifist, but they set up "a spiritual temple" kind of life on the outskirts of society as they waited for God's intervention. In the final eschatological battle they intended to take part and to occupy Jerusalem and to set up pure worship in the Temple. They awaited a Messiah of Israel to lead them in battle against the Gentiles. One of their scrolls, *The War of the Sons of Light and the Sons of Darkness,* gives the battle plan for this Holy War against both the Gentiles and the "wicked of the covenant." Significantly, they are not mentioned in the gospels. However, their lifestyle was quite a contrast to that of Jesus who seems to have avoided the imagery of the holy war. In fact he regularly attended the temple although quite critical of its abuses.[27]

4) Pharisees

A fourth option and the one closest to that of Jesus was the way of the Pharisees. They remained in the mainstream of society and because they accepted Roman rule as a divine punishment were in the main, pacifist. Of a Pharisee back-

[26]Cf Sanders, *Jesus and Judaism,* p. 98.

[27]According to Gerhard Lohfink, *Jesus and Community* ([New York: Paulist, 1984], pp. 26ff), Jesus was mainly concerned not so much with founding a Church as with the gathering and restoration of the people of God. But he understood the notion of the reign of God in such a universal way that he freed it from all national Jewish content. Thus in the Our Father the prayer is not for the liberation from Roman rule. Jesus rejected the Zealot approach, avoided that of the Essenes and fell into conflict with the restorative theology of the Sadducees, a conflict which led to his death.

ground, the historian, Josephus, used Deuteronomic theology to explain the disasters which befell the Jewish people. These were a divine punishment for the sins of a minor part of the people. He has Eleazer the leader of the Masada rebels declare: "We have been deprived, manifestly by God himself, of all hope of deliverance" because of his "anger at the many wrongs which we madly dared to inflict upon our countrymen."[28] The Pharisees, according to Josephus, attempted to dissuade the extremist zealots from launching their rebellion against Rome. Nevertheless, on at least two occasions they had refused allegiance to Herod and the Roman Emperor in the spirit of their tradition immortalized in the Book of Daniel. However, one prominent faction, the peace-seeking disciples of the Babylonian Pharisees (Hillel), although they did not accept the Herodian puppet regime, lived a peaceful life in agreement with the prophetic tradition of non-resistance to foreign oppressors (e.g. First Isaiah's attitude to the Assyrians, Jeremiah's to the Babylonians and Second Isaiah's to the Persians). In Hillel's view "the more charity the more peace" and so he exhorted his followers to:

> Be of the disciples of Aaron,
> loving peace, pursuing peace.
> Be one who loves his fellow creatures
> and draws them near to the Torah.[29]

5) Zealots

A fifth option which we shall consider in more detail because of its modern popularity is that of the terrorist or Zealot approach. A good description is found in the second and third volumes of the Jewish Wars of Josephus who held them responsible for the destruction of Jerusalem by the Romans. The Zealots regarded the Roman dominance as an affront

[28] *War* 7.331-3.
[29] *Aboth* 1:2.

against Yahweh to be removed by violent rebellion in the tradition of the Maccabees (1 Macc 2:26ff). After a brief reflection on the problem of terminology and a survey of some of the main scholars who have provoked the modern discussion, we will examine the pros and cons of the arguments for Jesus the Zealot.

The Zealots at the Time of Jesus

The common position among scholars[30] was that from 6 A.D., the rebellion of Judas the Galilean[31] against Rome's census until the suicide of the defenders of Masada in 74 A.D., there was in Palestine a rather monolithic resistance movement against Rome, with a clearcut ideology, a strict organization and a dynastic leadership, and a constantly growing level of violence. A number of modern scholars, granting the paucity of the available evidence, have suggested that this is a modern scholarly construct. No group known precisely as "the Zealots" seems to have existed until the second year of the great Jewish revolt of 66-70 A.D.[32] However, there were "several concrete

[30]Martin Hengel, *Die Zeloten. Untersuchungen zur Judischen Freiheitsbewegung in der Zeit von Herodes I bis 70 N. Chr.* (Leiden/ Koln: E.J. Brill, 1961); *Was Jesus a Revolutionist?* trans. William Klassen (Philadelphia: Fortress Press, 1971).

[31]Together with the Pharisee Zadok, Judas proclaimed that no other ruler except Yahweh alone should be recognized.

[32]Hernando Guevara, *La resistencia judia contra Roma* (Meitingen: Guevara, 1981): according to Josephus who wrote his history of the Jewish war "to commemorate the victories of his imperial patrons" and to show that the revolt did not reflect the true feeling of the Jewish people, Judas in association with a Pharisee named Zadok, founded a fourth philosophy in Judaism: "Its sectaries associated themselves in general with the doctrine of the Pharisees; but they had an invincible love of liberty, for they held God to be their only lord and master. They showed an indifference toward the fortunes of their parents and friends in their resolve to call no man master". (*Antiq* 18:23) Judas called the people cowards for consenting to pay tribute to Rome (*War* 2:36). But Josephus does not use the name Zealot for Judas' movement. He seems concerned to show that the Zealots were not true Jews but mere brigands and criminals. J. Massyngbaerde Ford (*My Enemy is My Guest,* p. 11) describes the zealot party as "probably a democratic body

movements led by figures recognized as kings, movements and leaders who actually ruled certain areas of the country for a time."[33] At least five resistance groups can be distinguished in the writings of Josephus:[34]

> a) the Sicarii, from the Latin word 'sica' meaning literally 'dagger people' or assassins, began their terrorist activity in the 50s. Their origin can perhaps be traced to Judas the Galilean's revolt in the so-called Fourth Philosophy which he founded. They lasted until Masada.
> b) The Zealots, a group who occupied the temple led by the priest Eleazer.
> c) The followers of the Galilean, John of Gischala, who were allied with the Zealots and who terrorized Jerusalem.[35]
> d) The followers of Simon bar Giora who controlled Southern Judaea and who fought against the Zealots.[36]
> e) The Idumaeans, who were variously allied with groups b) and c) and finally d).[37]

Whatever the terminology and the problems involved, the position taken here is that the option of Zealotry or armed resistance was a real option at the time of Jesus and indeed a tendency in the human situation in every age. The memory of such revolts as that of the Maccabees was well known in Judaism. Quite probably many of these groups shared the zeal

---

composed of lower-class priests, lay persons from Jerusalem, and small farmers, including 'bandits' from the countryside who appeared as a recognizable faction in 67-68."

[33] Richard A. Horsley, "Popular Messianic Movements Around the Time of Jesus," *CBQ* 46 (1984), pp. 471-495, p. 472.

[34] H. Merkel, *The Interpreter's Dictionary of the Bible,* supplementary vol., ed. George A. Buttrick (New York: Abingdon, 1962), p. 979.

[35] *War* 4.5.3.

[36] *War* 4.9.11.

[37] *War* 4.4.1.

for the Law which revived in the Maccabean period.[38] However, one must distinguish carefully these Zealot movements from many modern left-wing secular and marxist movements. As Martin Hengel[39] has carefully pointed out, figures like Judas the Galilean and Menahem were not only freedom fighters and leaders of armed bands, they were eschatological preachers of repentance with a tone of prophetic invective. The dividing lines between such figures and the Pharisees were fluid. Prior to 70 A.D. the Pharisees had a left wing influenced by charismatic eschatological tendencies. The school of Shammai in particular seems to have inclined towards the Jewish freedom movement.

The trouble with the Zealots of every age and their theocratic model, is that they have little real understanding of the complexities of a modern state. They tend to create more problems than they solve. According to M. Hengel[40] the Jewish religious Zealots under both Hasmonean and Roman rule failed to understand the need to "have control of an army with modern equipment and an effective administrative and financial apparatus, and to participate in a competitive way in world trade." The only possible form of state was the Hellenistic monarchy or city state. Refuge in a mythical past or apocalyptic future was no solution to their problems. The destruction of Jerusalem and widespread suffering were the fearful price which had to be paid for the unsuccessful rebellions of 66-74 and 132-135 with their dreams of utopian theocracy. According to Hengel, only the liberal wing of Pharisaism led by the

[38]According to Josephus the followers of Judas let neither torture nor death, friends nor families stand in the way of what they recognized as the will of God. The Jewish war began when the Temple captain Eleazer, a son of the former High Priest, joined the Zealots and soon afterwards murdered his father (*Antiq* 18:23; *War* 2:40ff).

[39]Martin Hengel, *Nachfolge und Charisma. Eine exegetisch-religionge-schichtliche Studie zu Mt 8.21f. und Jesu Ruf in die Nachfolge* (Berlin: Verlag Alfred Topelman, 1968); *The Charismatic Leader and His Followers*, trans. James Greig (New York: Crossroad, 1981), pp. 23f.

[40]*Jews, Greeks and Barbarians* (Philadelphia: Fortress Press, 1980), p. 81.

School of Hillel, showed "a viable way" forward, the way of obedience to the Law without self-destructive, political ambition. They clearly recognized that as long as God allowed the rule of Hellenistic Roman power, the godless "fourth empire" to endure, the politics of Israel was not of this world.[41]

The Zealot Hypothesis:
H.S. Reimarus (1694-1768)

The essay on *Jesus and his Disciples'* Purpose by Reimarus, the Hamburg Professor of Oriental languages, is generally recognized as the first landmark of research on the life of Jesus and in particular his political involvement.[42] As a young man, Reimarus had travelled in England and while there came in contact with deistic thought. For the Deists reason was a sufficient guide. Not surprisingly, Reimarus' *Apology for Rational Worshippers of God,* was critical of the morality of several Old Testament characters, the miracles, the resurrection accounts and any kind of religion which demanded belief in a particular revelation as necessary for salvation.[43] Reimarus went further than the moderate Rationalists who considered the essence of Christianity as synonymous with natural religion. Not only was Christianity based on revelation but its records were written by people motivated by dishonesty and fraud. Reimarus is thus the modern founder of the cover-up theory applied to the gospels. He proposed that Jesus' disciples, who did not want to go back to fishing for a living, fabricated the idea of Jesus as a spiritual Messiah after his unexpected

[41] Ibid., p. 82.

[42] Reimarus, *Fragments,* ed. C.H. Talbert (Philadelphia: Fortress Press, 1970); cf. E. Bammel and C.F.D. Moule, eds., *Jesus and the Politics of His Day,* (Cambridge: University Press, 1984).

[43] In the third of his posthumously published *Fragments,* Reimarus pointed out the historical impossibilities in accepting the Ex 12:37f text describing the passage of 600,000 men plus their wives, children, dependents and animals through the Red Sea. This would mean a total of three million who could not have crossed in a single night. Marching ten abreast they would have formed a column 180 miles long and would have required a minimum of ten days for the crossing.

death. Basing his opinion on the accusation that the disciples stole Jesus' body (Mt 28:11-15), so that the claim of an atoning death, a bodily resurrection and a second coming could not be disputed, Reimarus claimed that

> the system of a suffering spiritual saviour, which no one had ever known or thought of before, was invented only because the first hopes had failed.[44]

Both John the Baptist's and Jesus' ministry were calls to political revolt. When Jesus sent out messengers to announce the coming of the kingdom

> He knew that if the people believed his messengers, they would look for a worldly king, and would attach themselves to him with the conviction that he was this king.[45]

However, Jesus refused the attempt to make him king in a desert place (Jn 6:16):

> It was not his intention to allow himself to be made king in a desert place, and by a common rabble, such as then surrounded him. His thoughts were bent upon a grand entry into the city of Jerusalem, at the Passover, a time when all Israelites throughout Judea would be assembled there, and when it would be conducted in a festive manner, and when, by the united voices of the populace he would be proclaimed King of the Jews.[46]

However, in Jerusalem only the rabble accepted him and so Jesus lost his nerve:

> He ordered swords to be procured to defend himself in case

[44]Ibid., p. 151.
[45]Ibid., pp. 136ff.
[46]Ibid., pp. 142ff.

of attack, but was uneasy, lest even one of his own disciples should divulge his place of retreat. He began to quiver and quake when he saw that his adventure might cost him his life. Judas betrayed his hiding place ... He ended his life with the words, 'Eli, Eli, lama sabachtani? My God, my God, why hast thou forsaken me?' (Mt 27:46)—a confession which can hardly be otherwise interpreted than that God had not helped him to carry out his intention and attain his object as he had hoped he would have done. It was clearly not the intention or the object of Jesus to suffer and to die, but to build up a worldly kingdom, and to deliver the Israelites from bondage. It was in this that God had forsaken him, it was in this that his hopes had been frustrated.

This political-revolutionary dimension to Jesus' activity provoked many echoes such as Goethe's statement in 1814:

> ... the Christian religion is an intended political revolution which after failing, subsequently became an ethical one.[47]

Julius Wellhausen (1844-1918)

In his introduction to the first three gospels (1905), Julius Wellhausen, who was the most influential Old Testament scholar of his time, reflected on Reimarus' views. Considering the political expectation of the times and the violence at the cleansing of the temple and at his arrest, he admits a certain validity to Reimarus' views and that there were quasi-zealot aspects to the gospels. Jesus was not only a teacher but also an agitator who did not hesitate to use violence at the temple as his disciples did when surprised in the garden. His aim was to free his people from "the yoke of hierocracy and nomocracy."

Albert Schweitzer (1906)

The famous humanitarian missionary, Albert Schweitzer in *The Quest of the Historical Jesus,* surveyed the quest since

---

[47]Bammel and Moule, *Jesus and Politics,* p. 13.

Reimarus. He accused his nineteenth century predecessors of modernising Jesus to produce a projection of their own philosophical and theological ideas.[48] But he agreed with Reimarus that Jesus had failed to achieve his intended aim and that the gospel portrayal was different from the historical Jesus. For Schweitzer, Jesus' purpose from beginning to end was

> to set in motion the eschatological development of history, to let loose the final woes, the confusion and the strife from which shall issue the Parousia (p 371).

Not surprisingly, many who were anxious for social revolution claimed Jesus as one of their own. For W. Weitling (1845), Jesus, like Pythagoras was striving for a radical revolution in the social condition of his time and for the abolition of private property.[49] For the socialist, Karl Lautsky who wrote at the beginning of the century and who preferred Luke to the revisionist Matthew, what is most characteristic about Jesus is his rebellious mentality which was directed against both the Jewish and Roman establishments. This explains his execution, which otherwise would be an act of senseless wickedness, although it was played down by later tradition. Luke 12:49 and 22:38ff indicate a planned revolt after his successful assault on

---

[48]A series of articles against the dangers of excess, whether of the right with Barth or the left with Bultmann, as they tried to directly confront contemporary society with the kerygma, were written by the Quaker Henry J.Cadbury, "The Peril of Archaizing Ourselves," "Luke and the Horse-Doctors" (*The Journal of Biblical Literature* 52 [1933]: 55-56), and particularly, "*The Peril of Modernizing Jesus*" (London: SPCK, 1937). The last is a warning against attributing to Jesus an intention which had results in revolution, an argument directed both against Schweitzer and the views of Jesus as a social or political reformer. He sees Jesus' life as characterized by "an unreflective vagabondage" since "to plot a career de novo would occur to almost nobody" in Jesus' day. The absence of a definite unified conscious programme suits the historical evidence best. Sanders, *Jesus and Judaism*, pp. 19-22.

[49]For a detailed account of such claimants, cf. Bammel and Moule, *Jesus and Politics*, pp. 14ff.

the Temple, but his betrayal led to his downfall. Jesus' milieu was the rural proletariat. He called the poor because they were poor, and expected violent action from them. His Christian followers were essentially a city organization and therefore able to function as a secret society.[50]

Robert Eisler (1929-1930)

The first extensive treatment of Jesus as a political revolutionary was the two-volume study of the Austrian Jewish scholar, Robert Eisler, a study which caused enormous controversy. The title of the work, which is in the Greek language, can be translated into English as *Jesus, a King not Reigning,* with the significant sub-title *According to Flavius Josephus.* It includes the recently discovered 'Capture of Jerusalem' and other Jewish and Christian sources.[51] Eisler, taking up a quo-

---

[50]Cf. Ibid., pp. 19f.

[51]Heidelberg, 1929-1930. Eisler's argument was restated by Paul Winter, in *On the Trial of Jesus* (Berlin: de Gruyter, 1961; 2nd ed. Berlin/New York: de Gruyter, 1974) and popularized by the American Jewish writer, Noel Carmichael in his Pelican volume, *The Death of Jesus* in 1962. According to Ernst Bammel (*The Death of Jesus,* Naperville: A.R.Allenson, 1970, 47), the points of contact between Eisler and Winter, who neither uses Eisler's name or sources, are the following: the Zealot inclination among the Disciples of Jesus, the more restrained attitude of Jesus himself, the Roman responsibility for trial and execution, the mitigating tendencies in the NT documents. Winter attempts to deny the existence of a formal Sanhedrin trial. The Jewish involvement was minimal and confined only to a few while there was no discord between Jesus and the Pharisees. The charge against Jesus was entirely political. The Evangelists, especially Mark, attempted to give the contrary impression by inventing the story of a Sanhedrin trial. Carmichael blends together Eisler and Winter with Eisler's influence predominating. His Jesus was reared in the circle of John the Baptist who had tried to organize a secession. Jesus tried to establish the kingdom by storming Jerusalem: "Jesus was the Herald of the Kingdom of God and he tried to take it by storm. In the strangely blurred and mutilated recollections of his career we can dimly discern the outlines of a visionary who was also a man of action and who attempted to set in motion the machinery of God's will. He was squarely in the tradition of the Jewish religious patriots, tortured by the crushing weight of the Roman Empire, who arose in Palestine and assaulted the Roman power and its vassals. We see his enterprise frustrated and himself undone;

tation from G.B. Shaw, mockingly alludes to those who give the impression that Jesus only made speeches but never proceeded to action. Drawing mainly on sources outside the gospels, he makes the revolutionary ambition and failure of Jesus the key issue in his study. His Jesus is somewhat of a reluctant patriot. Persuaded by his followers to lead an armed revolt against the Romans, he is captured and executed for rebellion. According to Bammel, Eisler's picture of Jesus against the background of the social unrest of his time is the following

> Jesus' approach is characterised by the attempt to pacify the world by a 'mere message' which is announced by the disciples sent out to perform the task. Their lack of faith is a challenge to him to advance to radical action, the renunciation of everything dear to men's hearts, the return to the desert of the time of the pilgrimage: 'not revolt but merely a breaking out.' This exodus is to happen via Jerusalem from where he will lead Israel back over the Jordan and erect the tent of the patriarchal period. At the same time he is aware of a fate of ignominy and death that he has to encounter. The activists among his disciples, on the other hand, make sure of ambivalent orders given by the master and, indeed, of the whole journey to Jerusalem in order to gather together a large following, to give the entry into the Holy City the appearance of a messianic proclamation and to stage the occupation of the Temple. Jesus is drawn into these events rather than having planned them himself.[51a]

S.G.F. Brandon (1967)

The most thorough elaboration of the theory of Jesus the Revolutionary is found in the writings of S.G.F. Brandon, especially his *Jesus and the Zealots: A Study of the Political*

his followers scattered and his movement, doubtless, drowned in blood. He ended like many others in Israel—in agony and death, a prey to the powers of the world" (p. 203).

[51a]Bammel, *The Death of Jesus*, pp. 33-34.

Factor in Primitive Christianity.[52] Brandon begins with the statement that

> Ironic though it be, the most certain thing known about Jesus of Nazareth is that he was crucified by the Romans as a rebel against their government in Judaea.[53]

Brandon summarises his somewhat rambling study of the life of Jesus the Zealot-sympathizer as follows:

> Believing that the kingdom of God was at hand, Jesus sought to prepare his fellow-Jews morally and spiritually for membership of this kingdom, whose advent would achieve Israel's destiny as the Elect People of God. Two great obstacles stood in the way of the fulfilment of his mission: the Jewish sacerdotal aristocracy and the Roman government. Jesus seems to have been more concerned with

[52]A summary of Brandon's writings is found in my *Mark's Gospel* (New York: Paulist Press, 1982), pp. 151-153.

[53]Hengel himself agreed with J. Jeremias' judgement that Jesus was in the eyes of his opponents a false prophet and that as such he was handed over to the Romans with emphasis being put on his messianic claims. (Hengel, *The Charismatic Leader*, p. 42.) Significantly, S. Sandmel, *A Jewish Understanding of Jesus,* (Cincinnati, 1956), who is quite sceptical as regards the reconstruction of the historical Jesus, expresses his full agreement with Brandon's thesis (*Saturday Review,* 1969, p. 88). Sanders (*Jesus and Judaism,* p. 68) considers Brandon's view of Jesus sufficiently refuted by M. Hengel's *Was Jesus a Revolutionist?* (Philadelphia: Fortress, 1971). Also see J. Jeremias' *New Testament Theology.* London: SCM, p. 228. Brandon's thesis received little attention when he first proposed it in 1951. But the change in the political scene—the student revolutionary movements in 1968—and the more historical approach to the NT in addition to Brandon's further writings, led to a revival in the late sixties. James Barr (in the *Bulletin of John Rylands Library* (62 [1979-80]: 276), notes how Brandon told him of his surprise that people concluded from his writings that in imitation of Jesus we should support various groups of freedom fighters and other national/revolutionary movements in different parts of the world. Evidently, Brandon himself, who was an army chaplain during World War II, was quite conservative towards such movements and very much of the British Empire.

the former, probably because its members were Jews and the traditional leaders of Israel. Consequently, he saw their mode of life and abuse of power as constituting a scandalous contradiction of his ideal of a holy people, ready and prepared for the coming of God's kingdom. Their power, therefore, had to be challenged and perhaps broken. How long Jesus took in coming to this conclusion is not clear, but our sources point to his finally making a decision to go to Jerusalem, for action that he believed would be fateful. He carefully planned an entry into the city, which was designed to demonstrate his Messianic role. This challenging action was quickly followed by his attack on the Temple trading system ... the Jewish leaders did not then feel strong enough to arrest Jesus publicly. The operation in the Temple apparently took place about the same time as an insurrection elsewhere in the city, which the Romans suppressed ... it is difficult to believe that it was quite unconnected with Jesus' action in the Temple ....

What plans Jesus had, when he was arrested, are unknown. The fact that he was taken by night, after his rendezvous had been betrayed to the Jewish leaders by Judas, supports that he had no intention of surrendering himself voluntarily .... That Pilate sentenced him to death for sedition was the logical sequence to the case submitted by the Jewish authorities—that he also ordered him to be crucified between two ... who were probably Zealots, suggests that he connected Jesus with the insurrection that had coincided with Jesus' activities in Jerusalem.[53a]

For Brandon, Jesus was not strictly speaking a Zealot but a Zealot-sympathizer, ('with modification'), whose ministry had political dimensions. The whole New Testament, with Mark as the chief culprit, is a careful political coverup, a careful rewriting of history to conceal the fact that Jesus was a noble martyr for freedom. Mark's portrayal of an apolitical Jesus,

---

[53a] S.G.F. Brandon, *Jesus and the Zealots. A Study of the Political Factor in Primitive Christianity* (Manchester: University Press, 1967), pp. 350-351.

innocent of the charge of sedition, is expanded by Matthew and Luke into the concept of "the pacific Christ."[54] Mark, the first gospel to be written, is an *Apologia ad Christianos Romanos* and was written soon after the fall of Jerusalem in 70 A.D. It is an apology for Gentile readers in Rome where anti-Jewish sentiment was widespread. After the celebration of the conquest of rebel Judaea by Vespasian and his son Titus in Rome in 71 A.D., there was a most pressing need to avoid preaching a Jesus who was an executed Jewish freedom fighter and to explain Pilate's condemnation of Jesus.[55] According to Brandon, Mark's silence about the fall of Jerusalem is highly significant. Mark has no statement of hostility to the Romans or their representatives and in fact the climax of his story is the centurion's confession of faith (Mk 15:39). The enigmatic Mark 12:13-17 would have been read by a Roman audience as if Jesus supported the payment of tribute to Rome. Jesus is portrayed as essentially independent of his Jewish origin and relationships, as one who was never properly understood by the Jews. In fact he vehemently rebukes his chief apostle's obsession with a nationalistic conception of his person and mission. In Mark there is

> ... a consistent denigration of the Jewish leaders and people, and of the family of Jesus and the original apostles, which adds up to a damning indictment of the Jews for their treatment of Jesus ... the Jewish leaders and people are responsible for his death.[55a]

Brandon further argued that the Jewish Christians joined in the Zealot revolt and shared their fate when the Roman armies destroyed Jerusalem in 70 A.D. He insists that the supposed

---

[54]Ibid., pp. 283ff. Brandon considers Luke's three charges of perverting the nation, forbidding the tribute to Caesar and claiming to be a messianic king to be legitimate charges (Lk 23:2-5).

[55]Against Brandon's thesis is the absence in Mark of any trace of the Roman triumphs of Vespasian and Titus.

[55a]Brandon, *Jesus and the Zealots,* p. 279.

flight of the Christians before the siege to Pella is a later fabrication as it is not found until Eusebius and Epiphanius.[56]

A recent survey by John A. Ziesler[57] provides a very useful framework for an investigation of the problem. Like Aquinas he begins with the negative evidence, in five points. He concludes with the evidence against a Zealot-type of Jesus. I will follow the main lines of his argument in my next section.

---

[56]Eusebius *Ecclesiastical History* III, V 2-3.

[57]*The Jesus Question* (Lutterworth Press, 1980), p. 279.

2

The Case for a Zealot Jesus

1) Jesus' Proclamation of the Kingdom

In sharp contrast to our modern tendency to 'spiritualize' and emasculate such key biblical terms as justice, poverty and in particular kingdom, one must ask not so much how the evangelists later interpreted Jesus' message but how the ordinary people heard Jesus' kingdom message. The primary theme of Jesus' proclamation was the coming of God's kingdom (Mk 1:15). He insisted that this kingdom or ruling power and activity of God, which was partly present and partly future, was intimately bound up with his own person and activity. Although scholars may often have exaggerated the revolutionary atmosphere in Galilee,[58] it is quite probable that many of his contemporaries understood Jesus quite literally as if the political and religious kingdom was about to be restored to Israel and the Romans and their puppet Herods expelled.[59]

The extraordinary feeding of the five thousand in the wilderness naturally led to the conclusion that Jesus was a prophet like Moses the great liberator of the Jewish people (Deut 18:15ff). John has the same pattern as the synoptics in his chapter six, the feeding of a multitude, a walking on the water, a return to the west side of the lake, and a discourse on bread.

[58]Cf. Freyne, *Galilee,* pp 208-255.

[59]Lk 24:21; 13:1-2; Acts 1:6; 5:37.

Further he gives a vital clue not provided by the synoptics when he remarks that Jesus understood that the crowds had come to forcibly make him king. Unfortunately John does not give the account which we would like of this attempt to force Jesus to be their king. However, it is tempting to read the scene against the background of Mark. There the twelve have just returned from a mission in Galilee which had quite spectacular results, which had caught the attention of Herod Antipas who had recently killed John the Baptist. Jesus and the twelve withdraw out of Herod's territory across the lake, but the excited crowd of Galileans follow. Jesus teaches and feeds because he considers them to be "sheep without a shepherd." T.W. Manson insisted that these words did not mean a congregation without a pastor but an army without a captain.[60] Jesus well knew that a false captain like Judas could easily lead them to disaster.

2) Jesus Was Recognized as Messiah

Although there were quite a variety of messianic interpretations, the prominent one was Davidic, an interpretation which had strong religious and political connotations.[61] There is no evidence that Jesus used the title of himself during his earthly life. In three passages in Mark the use probably reflects the concerns of the early Christians.[62] However, the other three places in Mark where it is used, suggest that others saw in Jesus a political Messiah: Peter's confession at the key turning point in Mark's gospel at 8:29; the scribal claim that

[60] T.W.Manson, *The Servant-Messiah* (Cambridge: University Press, 1953), p 70; 1 Kgs 22:17; Num 27:17ff.

[61] Ps 18:51; 89:39, 52; 132:10, 17; Dn 9:25. Cf. Martin Hengel, *Between Jesus and Paul* (London: SCM, 1983), pp. 73f. Hengel is convinced that Jesus in his "messianic authority" gave the title Messiah a new interpretation which diverged markedly from the contemporary Jewish pictures of the Messiah.

[62] Mk 9:41; 13:21; 15:32.

the Messiah is David's son in 12:35; the high priest's question "Are you the Messiah?" in 14:62. If these are historical it seems quite logical to conclude that Jesus' lifestyle led people to believe that he would lead a political revolt. As Jesus marched towards Jerusalem, according to Luke's version, he sent before him thirty-six pairs of two into every town and place which he intended to visit (Lk 10:1ff). Certainly a fairly large scale expedition is involved if Luke's account is historical.[63] Further, the triumphal entry and cleansing of the Temple would have clearly recalled the previous triumphal cleansing of Jerusalem from foreign domination, by the heroic Judas Maccabeus.[64] It seems impossible that Jesus could have achieved what some scholars go so far as to describe as the occupation of the Temple without a considerable show of force, given the existence of the temple police and the Roman military presence in the Fortress Antonia which overlooked the Temple. Jesus' messianic action in the Temple was not only a blow at the Sadducee aristocracy who controlled the Temple and its sacrificial system but also at their Roman masters who installed and removed the High Priests at will. Within twenty years of Jesus' death when Paul began to write, the title Christ had become Jesus' proper name.[65] Cerfaux, who goes so far as to say that 'Christos' is the key term in the letters of Paul,[66] hesitates about this view. Yet he remarks that "the strikingly frequent use of the term to denote Jesus in Paul seems to be more of a riddle than a key to a better understanding of

---

[63] Michael Clevenot, *Materialist Approaches To The Bible,* (New York: Orbis Books, 1985), p. 138, identifies Mark's reference to Barabbas' uprising (Mk 15:7) with Jesus' entry into Jerusalem. He finds confirmation in W. Vischer's argument that the acclamation "Hosanna in the highest" is a transcription of the Hebrew HSNN BMRM. Vischer claims that by changing only one letter we have a subversive cry of the Zealots which would have been clear to the Jewish crowd but incomprehensible to the foreign soldiers: 'hsnn lmrm' which means "save us from the Romans."

[64] 1 Mac 10:1ff; Jn 10:32.

[65] Rom 9:5; Acts 2:36.

[66] Cf. Hengel, *Between Jesus and Paul,* p. 66.

Pauline Christology." There must have been some connection between Jesus' activity and this widely accepted title.

3) *Jesus' Crucifixion as a Revolutionary King*

The crucifixion is one great undisputed fact of Jesus' life apart from the much later Muslim denial. Jesus was crucified according to Pilate's title on the cross as "the King of the Jews" (Mk 15:26). The seeming contradiction involved in the execution of Jesus is well put by A.E. Harvey:[67]

> We are apparently faced with a contradiction. On the one hand, the events and legal procedures leading up to Jesus' death can be established with reasonable certainty as implications of the bare statement that he was crucified; and the charge upon which he was crucified is given by a report which, again, seems highly reliable: King of the Jews. On the other hand, it seems incredible that the person condemned on this charge was Jesus of Nazareth.

William Temple's famous criticism of the modern portraits of Jesus by liberal Protestants at the turn of the century is worth repeating:

> Why any man should have troubled to crucify the Christ of liberal Protestantism has always been a mystery.

A careful examination of the gospels can lead to the conclusion that despite his secret planning and careful preparations the rising failed. Jesus was arrested in the garden although he attempted to hide his presence there. Evidently Jesus' followers were armed and prepared to resist his arrest at Gethsemane with arms:

---

[67]A.E. Harvey, *Jesus on Trial. A Study in the Fourth Gospel* (London: SPCK, 1976), p 3.

> You have come out to arrest me armed with swords and clubs as if against a brigand (Mk 14:47); ... the man without a sword must sell his coat and buy one ... Lord, shall we use the sword? (Lk 22:36-49).

According to John 18:3, Jesus was arrested by a (Roman) cohort together with members of the temple guard (7:32). He uses the Greek word *speira* which is the technical equivalent of the Latin word *cohors* thus indicating that Roman soldiers were involved. Such cohorts were stationed in the Antonio Fortress at the northwest corner of the Temple. In theory, a cohort had a thousand soldiers and was commanded by a military tribune (Ac 21:31). Thus John indicated the importance of the arrest and the large number of troops required. According to the famous Albert Schweitzer in his *Quest of the Historical Jesus,* what Judas had betrayed to the chief priests was Jesus' self-claim and the belief of his small band that he was king. This provided the charge which they could present to Pilate. Jesus had to be got rid of. He clearly died on a political charge because the powers both civil and religious feared him, his values and his influence. Crucifixion was the punishment for political activity and especially rebellion.

4) Jesus the Zealot Associate and Sympathizer

The famous call of the Maccabees "Let everyone who is zealous for the Law and who takes his stand on the covenant come out and follow me" (1 Macc 2:27) has many echoes in Jesus' dealing with his followers. His so-called intensification of the Torah, such as his call to a renunciation of possessions,[68] his exhortations to martyrdom (Mt 5:10-12) were similar to the exhortations of contemporary apocalyptic and zealot type organizations. The image of carrying the cross could have come from a zealot background. By Jesus' time crucifixion

---

[68]Mt 6:19-25; 10:9-12; 19:16ff.

was a familiar Roman punishment for zealots.[69] John 2:17 applies the notion of zeal to Jesus when he quotes Psalm 69:10 concerning the cleansing of the Temple.

It is amazing how little we know about Jesus' closest associates. However, at least one of his disciples, Simon, was a zealot according to Lk 6:15. In Mk 3:18 and Mt 10:3 he is called the Cananaean which is quite likely a Greek transcription of the Aramaic (canana) meaning 'zealous.' Mark, who normally translates his Aramaic words, surprisingly does not translate this one. The suggestion is often made that only Luke who is at a safer distance from the Jewish revolt feels free to give the proper translation. Quite possibly other disciples were zealots also, such as James and John, nicknamed "sons of thunder," Judas Iscariot whose name can be derived from *sicarius* ('assassin') and even Peter whose surname 'Bar-Jona' has been interpreted somewhat unlikely as "zealot." Quite likely such people did not cease their zealot-sympathies on becoming disciples. Further, Jesus, who often criticizes different sects in Judaism ("Woe to you Pharisees") never seems to criticize the zealots directly. Not only did some of his disciples likewise carry arms (Lk 22:35-38) but Jesus' ideals of justice such as his proclamation of the Jubilee Year with its emphasis on freedom, on redistribution of land and cancelling of debts and also his criticism of power politics must have been close to the zealots' ideals.[70]

5) A Gospel Cover-up

The idea that the gospels are a cover-up portrayal of the historical Jesus is very much in keeping with the modern hermeneutic of suspicion and hidden agendas. The gospels were written from thirty to fifty years after the death of Jesus in different Christian communities such as Rome, Antioch,

---

[69] M. Hengel, *The Charismatic Leader and His Followers* (New York: Crossroad, 1981), p. 58.

[70] Lk 4:19; 6:24; 12:16-21; 13:32; 16:19-31; Mk 10:17-25, 44ff.

Greece and Asia Minor. No longer were the political problems of Palestine very relevant. The Christians were settling down and concerned with survival in the Roman Empire. They had no desire to have themselves or their founder portrayed as rebels against the mighty Roman Empire.[71]

No one could deny that Jesus was executed as a rebel. The approach of the evangelists was to show that the charge was unjust and that likewise Christians were politically harmless.

---

[71] Mark was writing in Rome not many years after Nero made the Christians bear the responsibility for the fire of 64 which the crowd blamed on himself. The Roman historian, Tacitus, gives an unforgettable description in his Annals 15:44:

"In order, if possible, to remove the imputation (that Nero had started the fire), he determined to transfer the guilt to others. For this purpose he punished, with exquisite torture, a race of men detested for their evil practices, by vulgar appellation commonly called Christians.

"The name was derived from Christ, who in the reign of Tiberius, suffered under Pontius Pilate, the procurator of Judaea. By that event the sect, of which he was the founder, received a blow, which, for a time, checked the growth of a dangerous superstition; but it revived soon after, and spread with renewed vigour, not only in Judaea, the soil that gave it birth, but even in the city of Rome, the common sink into which everything infamous and abominable flows like a torrent from all quarters of the world. Nero proceeded with his usual artifice. He founded a set of profligate and abandoned wretches, who were induced to confess themselves guilty, and, on the evidence of such men, a number of Christians were convicted, not indeed, upon clear evidence of their having set the city on fire, but rather on account of their sullen hatred of the whole human race. They were put to death with exquisite cruelty, and to their sufferings Nero added mockery and derision. Some were covered with the skins of wild beasts, and left to be devoured by dogs; others were nailed to the cross, numbers were burnt alive; and many, covered over with inflammable matter, were lighted up, when the day declined, to serve as torches during the night.

"For the convenience of seeing this tragic spectacle, the emperor lent his own gardens. He added the sports of the circus, and assisted in person, sometimes driving a curricle, and occasionally mixing with the rabble in his coachman's dress. At length the cruelty of these proceedings filled every beast with compassion. Humanity relented in favour of the Christians. The manners of that people were, no doubt, of a pernicious tendency, and their crimes called for the hand of justice; but it was evident, that they fell a sacrifice, not for the public good, but to glut the rage and cruelty of one man only."

The Roman leaders in Palestine had been fooled by the Jewish religious leaders who had seen Jesus as a religious threat to themselves. Recent scholars have pointed out the tendency of the four evangelists to whitewash the Romans and shift the responsibility for Jesus' execution from the Romans to the Jewish leaders. Central to this apologetic is the characterization of Pilate and his relations with the Jewish leaders. Pilate is described as concerned with justice but weak-willed in his relations with the troublesome Jewish authorities.

According to Mark, the first gospel, Pilate suspects the Jewish leaders of envy. Only with reluctance does he release Barabbas (whose name significantly seems to mean 'son of abba') and hand Jesus over to be crucified (Mk 15:10, 14). Matthew adds the dream of Pilate's wife who intercedes on behalf of the just man, Jesus. Further he has the episode where Pilate washes his hands of Jesus' death and the Jewish people accept the responsibility for it (Mt 27:18-25). Pilate, according to Matthew, insists that he is innocent of Jesus' blood. In Luke, Pilate not only three times pronounced that Jesus is innocent of any crime but proclaims that Herod, to whom he sent Jesus for his opinion, agrees with the judgement (Lk 23:4-22). Likewise, in John's gospel Pilate openly pronounced that Jesus is innocent of any crime (Jn 18:36; 19:4ff).

3

The Evidence Against a Zealot Jesus

A review of proposals like Brandon's will quickly show that a certain selectivity is at work in his case-building. Whatever passages help to build up his pre-determined position, he accepted. On the other hand, contrary evidence is too easily attributed to the cover-up of the early Church and its rather precarious position in the post-70 period in different parts of the Roman Empire. One should at least grant the possibility that such scholars are quite capable of reading their own prejudices into the gospels.

1) The Kingdom-Proclamation of Jesus

Granted that the kingdom was a central theme in Jesus' preaching it does not follow that its meaning was self-evident to his audience as Schweitzer assumed. Jesus is presented as taking over a traditional Jewish idea while giving it a new dimension in his teaching and deeds. However, as far as we can see he did not define 'kingdom' in discursive speech.[72] Neither did Paul. Even a brief survey of modern scholars

---

[72]Sanders, *Jesus and Judaism,* p 126; Joseph A. Fitzmyer, *The Gospel According to Luke (I-IX). Introduction, Translation, and Notes* (Anchor Bible 28) (Garden City, N.Y.: Doubleday and Company, Inc., 1981), pp 557, 154.

shows their difficulty in agreeing on a self-evident meaning for the term and in particular in discovering its nuance and range. However, the general meaning "the ruling power of God" is quite evident.[73] The simple fact is that although the kingdom is in some sense present and in another future, the same term is used to cover a wide range of meanings in both Paul and the synoptics.

The gospels show a Jesus who took great pains to expound the different dimensions of his view of the mystery of the kingdom, a mystery nonetheless. His call to a change of thinking and direction (repentance), his invitation to become like little children, his general life-style and behaviour have led many scholars to conclude that Jesus fitted in with no 'name' in Judaism and that he was not satisfied with any of the accepted philosophies of his day.[74] In his critique of all Israel he was like John the Baptist, though with a different approach and attitude and above all a sense of patience.

Jesus' view of the mysterious kingdom is essentially an invitation to believe, to trust, as the apocalyptic tradition insisted that God is in control. His approach is not so much a programme for action or a statement of human possibilities as a confident proclamation of God's mysterious intentions. He does not summon his disciples to bring in the kingdom. There is no statement that people can build the kingdom, rather it can be entered, received as a gift, or discovered like a pearl (Mt 13:44-46). The parables of the seed mysteriously growing "of itself" or "automatically," as the Greek word used translates, a parable found only in Mark (4:26-29), insists that it is God who will bring in his kingdom in his own time and without human worry or help. Like a farmer one can only wait in awe as the seed grows "he knows not how." The patience of the farmer is an example of the trustful waiting required of every Christian. This seems to be a criticism of those over hasty political agitators such as the Zealots who

---

[73]Sanders, *Jesus and Judaism,* p. 127.

[74]Kealy, *Who is Jesus of Nazareth?,* pp. 88ff.

want instant solutions to complex issues and who hope to establish the kingdom with the sword. Revolutionaries, it can be said, are those who believe they will solve more problems than they will create.

Jesus' reply to the Baptist's seeming criticism of his rather gentle approach seems to invite John to look at the good things that are happening, the signs of the kingdom which are all around,[75] in his service to the poor, the rejected, the outcast sinners. The temptation scenes stress that there are no easy instant solutions to the human predicament. Jesus further insists that his followers should not be involved in the usual power game of politics. As Matthew points out in a famous parable, it is not possible to make a clear cut distinction between the wheat and the weeds in this life (Mt 13:24ff). Reconciliation and forgiveness are at the heart of Jesus' approach because all are sinners, as they are reminded in the key prayer, the Our Father. A Christian is a lifelong learner or disciple in the school of failure. A kingdom disciple is like a sower sowing seeds, a rather humble occupation in which there is much failure and little instant success. Yet God does give the ultimate success.

2) *Jesus as Messiah*

The title "Messiah" could imply a revolutionary political leader. Yet a study of the evidence available shows that the term was variously used and that there was no clear-cut or consistent usage of the term in Jesus' day. Further, the expectation of an 'anointed' man of God was neither essential nor necessary in the expectations of the Jewish groups whose literary remains survive.[76]

---

[75] Lk 7:18ff; 11:20; 17:20f.

[76] Horsley, "Popular Messianic Movements," p. 494. Psalms of Solomon 17 clearly demonstrated that it is not accurate to reduce first-century Jewish messianic expectations to purely political terms or to the idea of a national warrior hero. Further, as B.S. Childs (*Introduction to the Old Testament as Scripture*) [Philadelphia: Fortress Press, 1979], p. 241) points out, it has long

According to the gospels, especially the earliest gospel Mark, Jesus seems to have avoided the title during his lifetime. Ironically, therefore, it became after his death the name by which he has been known ever since, Christ. The title Messiah is found eight times in Mark (Matthew seventeen; Luke twelve), i.e. 1:1,34; 8:29; 9:41; 12:35; 13:21; 14:61; 15:32. Most scholars agree that if the use of the title goes back to Jesus, that he used it or referred to it with great reserve. Whatever about the use of the title it seems clear, as Martin Hengel points out,[77] that he was not a popular messianic leader like Judas the Galilean or Theudas. He never called the people as a whole to follow him but he did expect all to repent. Nor did he make them all his disciples. He only selected some individuals. There is no trace of the idea of a Holy War as espoused by the Maccabees, Essenes and Zealots or that he could 'force' the coming of the final kingdom.

The kingdom was not so much something growing within history as something which comes as a gift of God independent of all human impatience and history (Mk 4:28). Jesus struggled against the demonic powers which enslaved people. But his only weapon was the word of authority with no hint of violence involved. However, this does not at all mean that Jesus made no messianic claims. For, as Hengel rightly points out[78]

> ... had Jesus not made messianic claims, not only his actions and his fate, but also the rapid development of

been recognized that, in its technical NT sense of the eschatological redeemer of Israel, the term 'messiah' does not occur in the OT itself but only in the post OT period. Cf. Sigmund Mowinckel, *He That Cometh* (Oxford: Blackwell, 1956), p. 4.

[77] *The Charismatic Leader,* p. 59; cf. Sanders, *Jesus and Judaism,* p. 307. For Sanders, there are only two places in the gospels in which Jesus accepts the title Messiah—the trial (Mk 14:61f) and Peter's confession (Mk 8:29f and pars.) and both are dubious historically. Further, the criterion of dissimilarity excludes the title from the ministry of Jesus because it was used by the early Church.

[78] *Between Jesus and Paul,* pp. 178f.

christology after Easter would be completely incomprehensible.

For Hengel[79] the basic problem of earliest Christology is not only how did Jesus become the Messiah but

> how did it come about that within a relatively short time—
> for religious developments in antiquity—the title Messiah
> came to be so closely associated with the name Jesus that it
> could not only be added to Jesus as a cognomen but could
> even take its place, and therefore is used by the first Chris-
> tian writer as the most frequent designation of Jesus.

The pivotal scene of Peter's confession (Mk 8:29) shows that Jesus was not publicly recognized as Messiah at that point of his ministry but as one of the prophets. Peter's insight is not denied but is corrected as Jesus' mission is more carefully defined in the light of the servant prophecies, as Mark 10:45 openly proclaims. In Mark 14:62 Jesus gives a clear affirmative answer to the high priest's question: "Are you the Messiah?" but both Matthew and Luke give a more evasive answer: "You have said so . . .".[80] Thus the evidence does not allow us to conclude that Jesus was a zealot from his messiahship. The book of Acts has two very interesting texts. Acts 2:36 suggests that Jesus was made by God to be Messiah after the resurrection. Acts 3:20, which has been called the oldest Christology preserved in the New Testament, relates Jesus' messiahship more to his future coming at the parousia than to his past activity on earth.

Can one interpret the triumphal entry as an armed entry and an occupation of the temple? The historian Josephus, who claims to give a comprehensive account of Jewish reactions to the Roman rule, does not mention it. Nor does Mark our oldest gospel describe it as such. Has he watered down the

---

[79] *Ibid,* p. 66.
[80] Mk 26:64; Lk 22:67-70.

event? Or rather, has he exaggerated the extent of Jesus' activity? Normally when there was a disorder the temple police and the Roman garrison in the Fortress Antonia which overlooked the temple would have quickly intervened. Jesus' action was against the Jewish priesthood and their administration of the Temple, not directly against the Romans (Mk 11:17ff). No one was killed! Further, an army would have been necessary to halt the trade required for the normal temple activities and there is no evidence for such a conflict. Sanders concludes his enquiry:

> It is reasonable to think that Jesus (and conceivably some of his followers, although none are mentioned) overturned some tables as a demonstrative action. It would appear that the action was not substantial enough even to interfere with the daily routine; for if it had been he would surely have been arrested on the spot. Thus those who saw it, and those who heard about it, would have known that it was a gesture intended to make a point rather than to have a concrete result; that is, they would have seen the action as symbolic.[81]

An interesting interpretation by Brandon is that Jesus' statement about giving to Caesar (Mk 12:13-17) was originally a statement of protest forbidding the payment of tribute to the Romans:

> It was, indeed, a saying of which any zealot would have approved, because for the zealot there was no doubt that God owned the land of Israel, not Caesar.[82]

For a faithful Jew there was really only one command: "There is one Yahweh and you shall love him with all your heart

---

[81] Sanders, *Jesus and Judaism,* pp. 70, 308. Sanders concludes from Josephus' description of a Zealot attack against the high priest and his guards (B.J. IV 300-18) which left 8,500 dead, that the temple even without Roman support was strongly defended (p 412).

[82] *Ibid,* p. 347.

.... " Only when the tribute saying is interpreted from a compromising point of view can it be seen as supporting the payment of any tribute to Caesar according to Brandon. A good summary of the three different modes of interpreting this very influential text is given in Joseph A. Fitzmyer's recent commentary on Luke's Gospel.[83]

a) The two kingdoms interpretation of Cullmann and von Ranke: This exists since patristic times and is aligned with late Jewish ideas.[84] It advocates paying the tribute to the legitimate claims of Caesar and includes a proper appreciation of the role of the state.[85] However, while the inaugurated kingdom does not supplant Caesar's, the danger is that there is a tendency to equate what is due to God and what is due to Caesar.[86]

b) The ironic interpretation of Schweitzer and Kierkegaard: Jesus' phrase "give to Caesar" is a flash of irony devoid of any serious importance. Even though the two parts of the sentence are joined by "and," the second part is adversative. Thus Jesus is not really interested in the tribute to Caesar. What is really important is what belongs to God.

---

[83]Fitzmyer, *Luke*, pp. 1292ff. The danger of Caesar's wanting to take all has ever been present particularly since the age of Constantine. Thomas More's reply to Henry VIII's claim to total sovereignty is famous: "I will obey you but swear total and absolute obedience—No." The unusual philosopher poet, Samuel Taylor Coleridge put the problem well when he described the role of the church as "the sustaining, correcting, befriending opposite of the world, the compensating counterface to the inherent and inevitable evils and defects of the state." Recently the London Cardinal Hume saw the constant role of the Church standing for the "things of God" in tension with the "things of Caesar" especially in the six areas of disparities of wealth, environmental deprivation, energy waste, nuclear war, hunger, neglect of basic human rights.

[84]Dan 2:21, 37-38; Prov 8:15-16; Wis 6:1-11.

[85]Ac 5:29; Rom 13:1-7.

[86]According to William Barclay (*The Plain Man's Guide to Ethics* [London: Fontana, 1973], p. 88), for Martin Luther, as individuals we must in the spiritual realm commit ourselves to the ethics of love while as citizens of the state we must accept the law of the state. Barclay concludes that there can hardly ever have been preached a more dangerous doctrine because on its basis at least a part of the German Church was able to accept Hitler.

c) The so-called anti-Zealot interpretation of Tertullian, Bornkamm and Schnackenburg: Thus Jesus openly opposes the refusal to pay the tribute but does not pronounce on the problem of the state. The coin which bears Caesar's image and which significantly "they" possess and use, not he, belongs to Caesar. People, because they bear God's image, owe themselves to God. Jesus does not set up two parallel but separate kingdoms, nor does he call in question Caesar's rightful kingdom. He insists not only that people are God's possession but that God has a claim to have his lordship recognized.

3) Jesus' Crucifixion as a Revolutionary King

According to Ziesler, Jesus was indeed crucified as a rebel but this was a miscarriage of justice due to Roman misunderstanding.[87] The trial accounts in the gospels are obviously telescoped summaries and far from the kind of evidence which we would like to examine in detail. It would be a misrepresentation to treat either the Gosepl accounts or the regulations for criminal cases found in the Mishnah as if they were actual case records or objective descriptions of the trial of Jesus. Both were written for quite different purposes. Obviously scholars can theorize and debate the historical details.

There is no clear statement why the Jewish leaders wanted the death of Jesus or why they had to persuade the Romans to

---

[87]John Ziesler, *The Jesus Question,* p. 34. Sanders (*Jesus and Judaism,* pp. 300-318), suggests that if we admit that the long trial scene of Matthew and Mark is not historical then we do not know if there was a trial, if the whole Sanhedrin actually convened, if there was a formal charge or a formal conviction under Jewish law. He rightly points out that trials and judgements need not have been carried out in the orderly fashion described in the Mishnah Sanhedrin. He concludes that the vaguer account of John seems better to correspond to the way things actually worked out. The situation seems to require only the involvement of the priests. Although he finds it difficult to discover any substantial conflict between Jesus and the Pharisees, he does not exclude the participation of the Pharisees because it is possible there was a Sanhedrin hearing and therefore the presence of the scribes.

condemn and execute him. E. Schillebeeckx[88] points out that the antagonism between the parties represented in the Jewish Sanhedrin, then under the presidency of the high priest, was too great in Jesus' time to get a consensus on condemning Jesus to death. Yet all members of the Sanhedrin had fundamental objections to Jesus of Nazareth. All would have agreed that in view of the rumours among the people, the Jesus affair was dangerous for the Romans. The religious and political dimensions were so intertwined that one could argue that Jesus was a political threat.

> What they could and did reach was a majority decision to go and hand over (for allegedly political reasons) a compatriot, Jesus of Nazareth, to the Romans—so much hated, as they were, by most of the Sanhedrin themselves![89]

Thus the title over the cross "the King of the Jews" could easily represent the Roman understanding of the Sanhedrin presentation of the case of Jesus to them even though they might not have understood the religious implications or perhaps cared to understand them.[90]

Raymond E. Brown[91] has distinguished four views usually presented on the problem of the involvement of the Jewish authorities.

a) The classical view sees the Jewish authorities as the prime movers.

[88]*Jesus,* New York: Seabury, 1979, pp. 313ff.

[89]*Ibid,* p. 317.

[90]Paul W. Walaskay, in his study of the political perspective of Luke, *And so We Come to Rome* (Cambridge: University Press, 1983), concludes that in contrast to his source, Mark, Luke seems to show that Pilate could not discover sufficient testimony to proceed with criminal charges—the Jews were not concerned to provide evidence for a legitimate trial. Thus Jesus is treated fairly but quite ineptly by the Roman political system. Yet the fact that Pilate allows himself to be overruled by the Jewish demands is not the kind of picture one would concoct to please a Roman audience.

[91]*John* (Anchor Bible 29) (Garden City: Doubleday and Company, Inc., 1966-70), p. 792f.

b) A modified view accepted by many Christian scholars suggests that despite deep involvement by the Jewish authorities, no Jewish sentence on Jesus was actually passed. All the main legalities were carried out by the Romans.

c) The Romans were the prime movers and Jewish cooperation was forced. Possibly a political Roman rubber-stamp Sanhedrin was involved but not the religious Sanhedrin or only a small clique but not the Pharisees.

d) No Jewish authorities were involved in any way even as a Roman tool. All such suggestions are an apologetic falsification of history. However, the oldest Jewish references clearly accept Jewish involvement in Jesus' death.

According to a recent study of the trial and death of Jesus[92] most of the Jewish scholars, who in recent times have studied the problems involved, posit some collaboration between elements of the Sadducean-controlled priestly circle connected with the Jerusalem Temple and the local Roman authorities. Further, they are unwilling to restrict Jewish involvement to the initial arrest and questioning. These Jewish leaders who were marked by a certain degree of corruption and financial gain, were not held in high respect by many others in Judaism particularly by the Pharisees. Thus the Jewish historian Ellis Rivkin writes:

> What crucified Jesus was the destruction of human rights, Roman imperialism, selfish collaboration . . . . If these were among the Jews who abetted such a regime, then they too shared the responsibility. The mass of Jews, however, who were so bitterly suffering under Roman domination that they were to revolt in but a few years against its tyranny, can hardly be said to have crucified Jesus. In the crucifixion, their own plight of helplessness, humiliation and subjection were clearly written on the cross itself. By nailing to the cross one who claimed to be the Messiah to free human

[92]John T. Pawlikowski O.S.M., in *Chicago Studies,* 24 (1986): pp. 88-97, 88f.

beings, Rome and its collaborators indicated their attitude towards human freedom.

The author of the survey, John T. Pawlikowski, concludes that rightly or wrongly Jesus was tried as a political rather than a religious agitator. Further, until we reassociate Jesus with the wider Jewish struggle of the times against spiritual and political oppression, the Church's celebration of Holy Week will continue to carry the seeds of anti-Semitism. However, the claim of some Jewish scholars that Jesus was an active revolutionary leader speaking out against Rome remains unproven on the available evidence. Nevertheless, Pawlikowski is convinced that

> Jesus was far more an activist than the portrayals of him in this regard by Christian exegetes such as Oscar Cullmann or Robert Grant or the depiction of his ministry found in the biblical section of the American Bishop's Peace Pastoral. But he probably confined his politics primarily to the internal structures of Judaism rather than mounting a frontal attack on Roman hegemony in Palestine. His threat to the establishment leadership of the Temple led to his arrest and death. Many other Jews shared his sentiment though they may have been less vocal.[93]

Pawlikowski sees the recent study *Jesus and Judaism*[94] as moving in the same direction. Sanders argues that

> it was Jesus' preaching against existing concepts of the Temple as the center of Jewish life and its invasion by him to dramatize his point that led to his execution at the hands of Rome with the urging of at least some of the priestly leaders.[95]

---

[93] *Ibid*, p. 91.

[94] Sanders, *Jesus and Judaism*, p. 91.

[95] *Ibid*.

Admittedly the sayings about swords and the incident in Gethsemane are difficult to explain. The statement "not peace but a sword" (Mt 10:34) seems clearly to be understood metaphorically. Likewise the famous passage about "the Two Swords" (Lk 22:35-38) is best understood metaphorically as inviting an apostle of Jesus to set out equipped with his kind of (spiritual) armour as he faces the inevitable persecution. Ever since John Chrysostom's commentary on Matthew there have been interpretations of the sword as a reference to the daggerlike butcher knife used for killing the Passover lamb. But the Greek word used 'macharia' designated a variety of swords. The passage is heavily ironic, insisting as it does on the blindness of the disciples. The question in Gethsemane "shall we strike with a sword?" and the cutting off of the ear are quite probably based on a historical reminiscence.

4) Jesus the Zealot Associate and Sympathizer

One can grant that some with Zealot sympathies joined Jesus' group. However, the argument from the term zelotes (Lk 6:15; Ac 1:13) is far from decisive. The word may mean simply 'enthusiast.' Further, the fact that Zealots joined his group does not mean that he agreed with them or that they continued in their belief. The Gospels insist on Jesus' call to continuing conversion and on the differences between Jesus' ideas and those of his disciples. In particular, one can point to a wide range of teachings and behaviour on the part of Jesus which would have been quite unacceptable to any self-respecting Zealot. Jesus, also called a tax-collector, a hated collaborator, and associated with tax-collectors, an association which would have been considered betrayal.[96] He spoke of loving one's enemies (Mt 5:44). He could even praise a Roman official—"I have never found this much faith in Israel"[97] and

[96] Mk 2:14-17; Lk 7:34; 15:1ff; Mt 11:19.
[97] Mt 8:5-13; Lk 7:1-10.

hold up a hated Samaritan as a model soon after he was rejected by a Samaritan village.[98] His criticism of much of the Pharisaic legislation and behaviour would have been quite offensive to many Zealots. In particular Jesus' radical approach with regard to the renunciation of violence would have been considered crazy by a Zealot.[99] There seems to be widespread agreement among New Testament exegetes that in the Q texts which insist on the renunciation of violence,[100] we hear the voice of Jesus himself speaking. The gospels do not use such terms as non-violence or non-resistance or treat the problem abstractly. Jesus was well aware of the use of power, force and physical coercion in his own country. His emphasis was much more on the power of love, forgiveness, compassion and generosity.[101]

[98]Lk 9:51ff; 10:25ff.

[99]According to Robert North, the German exegete, R. Schwager has discovered in the OT some 600 passages where violence is condemned in foreign kings or tribes or in guilty Israel. But a full 1000 texts focus on Yahweh's own violence and at least a few of these describe an irrational violence. Most of Yahweh's interventions which seem as capricious as "a drunk leaping up from sleep" (Ps 78:65) are quite simply "the fulfilment of nature's inexorable laws in relation to man's own irrational behaviour." For Schwager, the impact of these "Thousand Violences of Yahweh" is the "gradual emergence of a new community of peace and love already fore-shadowed in earlier episodes like the curiously chosen David and Jonathan." R. North, "Violence and the Bible: The Girard Connection," *CBQ* 47 (1985): 14-15.

[100]Mt 5:39-42; Lk 6:27-31.

[101]James McPolin in *Irish Challenges to Theology* ([Dublin: Dominican Publications, 1986], pp. 83f.) gives a good summary of the differences between Jesus and the Zealots:
"His demands concerning wealth are not merely based on some social programme. They are also linked with trust in the goodness of the Father (Mt 6:24-25). He set out to liberate Israel by persuading people to change (Mk 1:15). A way to be liberated from your enemies, he said, was to love them; do good to those who hate you, pray for those who treat you badly (Lk 6:27-28). This was not a matter of resigning oneself to Roman oppression nor was it a matter of trying to kill them with kindness. Rather, one had to reach down to the root cause of all oppression and domination: lack of compassion (Mt 18:35). If the people of Israel were to continue to lack

Important texts which bear on these issues are the eschato-logical discourses found in the three synoptics (Mk 13; Mt 24; Lk 21), texts which were quite influential in the life and be-haviour of the early Christians. Matthew 25 foretells a future of international tension and conflict, earthquakes, lawlessness, alienation in human relations, apostasy in the Church and worldwide distress. But there is no vision of a warlike inter-vention by the risen Jesus to liberate his people. Neither is there any suggestion that his followers should wage a holy war. Messianic liberators are expected to arise but Jesus' fol-lowers are warned against heeding their summonses. The emphasis is not so much on activism as on witness, on faith-fulness. Deliverance will be brought about by the coming of the Son of Man and his intervention from above. When he comes it will not be to initiate a war of liberation, still less of revenge. Rather, it will be a day of judgement, an impartial judgement not least of all on the Christians themselves.

5) A Gospel Cover-up

The suspicion of a cover-up is difficult to dispel. In theory everything which is contrary to a zealot-sympathizing Jesus could be due to a conspiracy of the early Christians trying to survive in the hostile Roman Empire. Critics of almost every age have tried to impugn the credibility of the gospel portrait of Jesus.[102] The most learned critic of Christianity in its early centuries was the formidable Porphyry. The vigour, scope and extent of his criticism must have stunned many early Christian

compassion would the overthrowing of the Romans make Israel any more liberated than before? If the Jews continued to live off the worldly values of money, prestige, group solidarity and power, would the Roman oppression not be replaced by an equally loveless Jewish oppression? Jesus was more concerned about Jewish liberation than the Zealots. They were fighting for Jewish nationalism, Jewish racialism, Jewish superiority and Jewish relig-ion."

[102]For a recent controversy consult, Gerald O'Collins, "Jesus and the Scholars," *The Tablet,* 13 October 1984, pp. 1002ff.

communities to judge by the many who tried to refute him from Eusebius, Methodius, Apollinarius to Augustine. Emperors such as Constantine and Theodosius II tried to have his writings burned. The key issue, as Porphyry stated, and as Augustine reiterated in his defense of the Scriptures, was the historical reliability of the gospel account of Jesus.[103] It was against such works as Porphyry's *Against the Christians* that Augustine wrote his *Harmony of the Gospels.*

In Brandon's earlier work, *The Fall of Jerusalem and The Christian Church,* he argues that there was a serious discrepancy between the teaching of the church in Jerusalem, which was in sympathy with zealotry, and the teaching successfully propagated outside Judaea by Paul and the other leaders of the Gentile mission. Brandon further develops this argument in his *Jesus and the Zealots,* trying to show that Jesus himself was a zealot-sympathizer. He rejected the second century tradition of the flight of the Christians to Pella, a Decapolis city some sixty miles from Jerusalem. This tradition had been a key factor in the theory that the Jerusalem Christians had refused to take part in the Jewish revolt against the Romans.[104]

However, as Ziesler points out, the evidence of Paul's letters tells decisively against Brandon's thesis. The excitable Paul is never shy in describing his many controversies. He was continually defending the gospels against wrong interpretation whether legalism, libertinism, incipient gnosticism, extreme asceticism. Paul even has difficulties with Peter's interpretation at times. But he never has problems in his wide travels with revolutionary nationalism. Romans 13 is the only passage in the authentic Pauline letters where attention is directly paid to the political authorities and to the relations of the Christians and the state. In this chapter Paul recommends submission but not unconditional obedience to the functionaries of the

---

[103]Robert L. Wilken, *The Christians as the Romans Saw Them,* (New Haven: Yale University Press, 1984), pp. 126ff. This study shows that in contrast to those who believe that critical intelligence arose with the Enlightenment, many of the issues were raised by critics many centuries ago.

[104]Eusebius, *Ecclesiastical History* III, V. 2-3.

imperial government. These verses have often been misunderstood and, in the words of J.C. O'Neill "have caused more unhappiness than any other seven verses in the New Testament because of the licence which they have given to tyrants."[105]

However there is no suggestion in Paul that the Christians were in any sense political revolutionaries. Ziesler gives two further reasons which make the zealot interpretation of Judaean Christianity highly unlikely. If the original Christians were nationalistic and focused on a zealot type political activity it is difficult to imagine how a Paul or gentiles in particular found it to be a good basis for a universal religion. Further, it seems that the Jewish Christians were quite harmless at least in Roman eyes. They were left alone after the death of Jesus. Apart from the radical Stephen and Paul's persecution there were few political problems. It was not until some thirty five years after Jesus' death that there was any state persecution. Nero's Roman persecution took place far from the land and problems of Palestine.

[105]Cf. Robert J. Daly, S.J., (ed), *Christian Bible Ethics* (New York: Paulist Press, 1984), pp. 266ff.

4

Conclusion

Prove Too Much?—A Soothing Baptizer of the Status Quo?

The danger in rejecting the zealot-sympathizing Jesus of Brandon's hypothesis is that one proves too much to produce a politically harmless Jesus, a gentle Jesus, meek and mild. Thus for Michael Clévenot[106] it is evident that Mark did not want to present Jesus as a Zealot Messiah.

> But it does not mean, as the traditional idealist exegesis claims, that Mark made him into a spiritual Messiah, abandoning the temporal domain to the jurisdiction of Caesar.

Clévenot's materialist reading sees in Jesus a strategy which he calls "communist, non-revolutionary, and internationalist." It was communist because it aimed at

> reestablishing sharing, the value of the use against the value of exchange.

---

[106]Clevenot, *Materialist Approaches to the Bible,* p. 92.

It was non-revolutionary

> because the economic and political conditions of the Jewish
> sub-Asian system integrated into a slave-holding Roman
> Imperial system did not permit a revolutionary transfor-
> mation of the relationships of production.

It was internationalist because

> the narrative constantly crossed the borders of Palestine
> and ended by bursting out towards Galilee in the direction
> of the pagan countries.

For Clévenot the very existence of Mark's text is evidence
that the narration of the practice of Jesus was in fact a message
of happiness at the time it was written down. It is a message
which must be seized from those who have never hesitated to
enclose it, to turn it into a Law, a heavy burden (Mt 23:4). As
its title indicates, *The Good News of Jesus the Messiah,*
Clévenot's explanation of the good news is found in the nar-
rative of the practice of Jesus which is gradually revealed to be
messianic,

> to liberate suffering and outcast bodies, to invite people to a
> life of sharing rather than the reign of money, to challenge
> the repressive power of class domination, to disclose the
> emptiness and sterility of the social system. The practice is
> indeed seen to rediscover the prophetic vein of Elijah, Elisha,
> Amos and Jeremiah. It is seen to inaugurate the messianic
> era of human relationships, which are finally reciprocal and
> fraternal.[107]

The problem was not so much with Brandon himself. He was
careful to point out that Jesus himself was no zealot although
there were political dimensions to his ministry. However, Brandon's problem lay in his thesis that the early Church, par-

[107] *Ibid.*, pp. 101ff.

ticularly the gospel of Mark, attempted to cover up these dimensions. Because Mark was writing in Rome, soon after the booty from Jerusalem was being carried through the streets of Rome in Titus' victory procession, he felt obliged to defend the political innocence of Jesus. Mark's apolitical Jesus was expanded by Matthew and Luke into "the concept of the pacific Christ."[108] However, the use of Brandon's findings as well as those of Winter and Eisler by such popularizers as J. Carmichael[109] had enormous impact in Germany through a discussion in the magazine *Der Spiegel*. According to this theory Jesus was brought up in the environment of John the Baptist who had led a secessionist movement from the Roman and Jewish authorities. Jesus in turn had broken with John and attempted to establish the kingdom, not in the desert but by storming Jerusalem. His movement was marked by violence, had anti-Roman political implications and ended in failure although he had occupied the Temple for a time aided by such subordinates as the two robbers who were later crucified with him. The turning point in Jesus' career was Pilate's defilement of the sanctuary by setting up Roman standards there, an event alluded to in Mark 13:14. Carmichael saw Jesus as part of the mainstream of Jewish life and denied any messianic consciousness to him.

In rejecting such theories the danger is to turn Jesus into a soothing baptizer of the status quo. Even a quick reading of a gospel such as Mark's shows a disturbing Jesus who was constantly engaged in controversies from the moment he closed his carpenter's shop to step into the public arena of Palestine. He was not only a surprise to the Judaism of his day but he succeeded in quickly alienating both the political and religious authorities of his time so that such strange bed fellows as the Pharisees and the Herodians plotted to destroy him (Mk 3:6; 7:1ff). He baffled even his own relatives (3:31-35) and offended the villagers of his native place (6:1-6). Then he withdrew from

---

[108]Brandon, *Jesus and the Zealots,* pp. 283-321.

[109] *The Death of Jesus* (Gollancz, 1963).

Galilee to severely criticize the ideas and values of his own disciples, even describing Peter as a devil (8:33). Jesus comes across as the African scholar, John Mbiti described him, as one who stands in judgement over the culture of every society and age. He is a disturber of the status quo of every person, a question mark by his words and lifestyle of the existing religious, social and political order of his time and ours, in almost every aspect. Jesus seemed to criticize everything from the possession of wealth to the way authority and leadership were exercised. He quickly bursts the bounds of any philosophy which tries to imprison him. He could differ from many aspects of the zealot philosophy, yet share their passionate concern for the coming of God's kingdom and the doing of God's will. According to Luke, his proclamation of good news to the poor and his Jubilee vision of liberation from fear to a more abundant life, from blindness to seeing with suffering humanity, from self-centredness to an attitude of detached giving, from vengeance to forgiveness was not acceptable to the poor themselves at Nazareth.[110]

Jesus' kingdom was no mere personal individual matter but, as a survey of the synoptic tradition shows, was concerned with community. Certainly, he did address individuals of a wide variety, male and female, rich and poor, Jew and occasionally Gentile. He clearly invited each person to decide in freedom and to grow in decision-making. But he was not concerned with a mere collection of individuals. Rather he sought to gather and restore the true people of God in community as the community prayer, the Our Father, shows.

Ernst Bloch

Scholars such as Ernst Bloch, a thinker characterised by an "atheism for God's sake," according to Moltmann's introduction to his work, *Man On His Own,* have compelled modern biblical scholars and liberation theologians to take a fresh and

---

[110]Seán P. Kealy, C.S.Sp., *Towards a Biblical Spirituality* (Dublin: Carmelite Centre of Spirituality, 1985), p. 56.

hard look at Jesus' actual bible with its paradigmatic event, the Exodus. This key event shows that Israel did believe in a this-worldly salvation. The Decalogue, a key Old Testament text begins:

> I am Yahweh, your God, who led you out of Egypt, out of the house of slavery.

Norbert Lohfink

Norbert Lohfink[111] points out that the Hebrew word for lead out, *hosi,* was a legal term meaning "to emancipate or free a slave." Later the message of Deutero-Isaiah was simple and concrete.

> Keep hoping, for your serfdom is coming to an end! Babylon will fall! You will become free, and be able to return home.

Thus, according to Lohfink, at the centre of the Old Testament preaching of redemption is liberation from foreign rule and forced labour, a healing of bodies not souls, the salvation of the nation and society and not merely the individual. None of this has been pushed aside by the New Testament to be replaced by a spiritualized other worldly hope. However, according to the Old Testament, it is Yahweh alone and never people who brings about the Exodus and the liberation of the world. Jesus with his command to "follow me" takes the role of Yahweh in the New Testament.

John A.T.Robinson

In a profound sense Jesus was far more radical than the revolutionaries of his or any subsequent age. In one of his talks, the late John A.T. Robinson made an interesting comparison between the reformer and the revolutionary and the radical.

---

[111] *Great Themes from the Old Testament* (Edinburgh, T & T Clark), p. 96.

The reformer is basically content with the system if only certain things can be improved such as laws, working conditions, etc. The revolutionary wants to tear up the system to begin again. Jesus accepted the institutions of Israel. He went regularly to the synagogue and the Temple and, as Luke insists, was a pious Jew in contrast to many of his opponents. Jesus was the radical who went to the roots. These were twofold: God and the human heart. The essential aim of Jesus was to fulfil whatever God wanted, as the opening words of Jesus in Matthew show. Typical of his questions were: why did God institute the sabbath for people or vice versa? what were God's requirements in marriage? Secondly, in keeping with many of the rabbis he insisted that God's commands were to be fulfilled with *kawwanah,* "inwardness" or from the heart, the interior, the seat of decision-making. God's will is to rule in the heart, to be the centre of all our lives and decisions.[112]

Martin Hengel

According to Martin Hengel[113] Jesus' teaching as a totality was presented with charismatic authority. He neither followed the rabbinical approach of deducing it from the Torah nor the approach of the wisdom teachers by appealing to the evidential force of his teaching based on observation and experience.

> The radicalized demand for love of one's neighbours, resulting in renunciation of violence and rejection of loveless ritualism; the pointlessness of worry and the unconditional nature of forgiveness; the condemnation of all self-assurance and self-righteousness; his whole 'ethical' preaching, can be seen as an eschatologically preconditioned expression of his charismatically based call to decision. The pressing forcefulness of this call is legitimately described by all three evangelists by their use of the term 'exousia' (Mk 1:22, 27).

[112] Jer 31:31-34; Ezek 11:17-21; 36:22-32; Joel 2:27-29.
[113] *The Charismatic Leader,* p. 67.

Milan Machoveč

Very often it takes an outsider to tell us how radical Jesus really was. Marxists have at last begun to look seriously at Jesus and Christianity. In fact one of the best studies of Jesus by a non-Christian comes from the convinced Marxist philosopher, the Czech, Milan Machoveč. His book has the English title, *A Marxist Looks at Jesus*,[114] a less attractive title than the German one, *Jesus for Atheists*.[115] It is the first socialist approach which dispenses with Marxist economic criteria. Machoveč rejects the picture of Jesus "Thou hast conquered, O pale Galilean and all the world has grown grey with thy breath" popularized by Swinburne.[116] His portrayal of Jesus shows positive sympathy and understanding both for his person and his message. He begins with the presupposition that Jesus was different from the established positions in contemporary Judaism and suggests that it would be surprising if he had not developed an entirely unique position on such questions as force. One should at least grant that Jesus was a person of tremendous vigour and dynamism with a remarkable power of drawing men and women to himself and holding their loyalty through good days and bad.[117] His doctrine set the world on fire

> not because of the obvious superiority of his theoretical programme, but rather because he himself was at one with the programme, because he himself was the attraction. They saw in him a man who already belonged to this coming Kingdom of God; they saw what it meant to be 'full of grace,' what it meant to be not only a preacher but himself the product of his preaching, a child of the future age to the marrow of his bones.[118]

[114]London, 1976.

[115]Stuttgart, 1972.

[116]Hymn to Prosperine, 1866.

[117]Machoveč, p. 81.

[118]Ibid, pp. 82ff.

For Machoveč, Christians so often make the harshest demands on others while absolving themselves

> though the principle of the 'speck in the eye of the brother' was one of the reasons which led Marx to accuse Jesus' followers of hypocrisy, double-dealing and Pharisaism. One must nevertheless acknowledge that something great and important entered human history through the message of Jesus .... That is why Jesus' demand for change, his conception of the eschatological call to conversion could for centuries be the basis for the intellectual history of the West from St. Augustine to Luther and Hegel.[119]

Christianity, according to Machoveč has produced a dogmatized image of Jesus Christ but has never succeeded in thoroughly banishing the image of the man Jesus of Nazareth:

> This has often been driven underground, preserved by saints or heretics who often were brought to the very limit of their human strength and possibilities because they asserted the meaning of Jesus' words against the authoritarian guardians of dead conventions.[120]

Machoveč has succeeded in portraying a much more radical Jesus than a zealot Jesus, one who embraced the whole person both inner and external, one who above all was concerned with the future, God's future which should totally control even the present. Characteristic of Jesus was his emphasis on activity without the use of force—"'love your neighbour' is an iron demand without any compromise towards yourself."[121]

Admittedly Machoveč's portrayal of Jesus with his hope against all hope, is utopian and perhaps influenced by his Bohemian religious heritage. However, the important thing is

[119]Ibid, pp. 111-112.

[120]Ibid, p. 203.

[121]Ibid, p. 110.

that for a Marxist in search of liberated persons he finds Jesus, "The Lord of the Dance" highly significant. Why, he is not afraid to ask, did the disciples after the unexpected death of Jesus continue their dance? Why did his cause not end at the cross? He dismisses such rationalistic explanations of the resurrection as mere visions, the stealing of the body as ungrounded in historical testimonies. That something happened which the Christians call Easter, Elevation or Resurrection and the consequences of which are historically verifiable seems to him to be beyond reasonable doubt. He concludes that, if the new liberated person is completely the result of changed forms of production, there is no real explanation of what changed the disciples at Easter.

H.G. Wells

The impact of Jesus has also been unforgettably summed up by the famous writer, H.G. Wells in his *Outline of History*.[122] He attempted to portray Jesus in such a way that he could be appreciated by Hindus, Moslems and Buddhists as well as Americans and Western Europeans. Summarising the impact of Jesus he concludes that:

> He was too great for his disciples and in view of what he plainly said, is it any wonder that all who were rich and prosperous felt a horror of strange things, a swimming of their world at his teaching? Perhaps the priests and the rulers and the rich men understood him better than his followers. He was dragging out all the little private reservations they had made from social service into the light of a universal religious life. He was like some terrible moral huntsman digging mankind out of snug burrows in which they had lived hitherto. In the white blaze of this kingdom of his, there was to be no property, no privilege, no pride or precedence, no motive indeed, and no reward but love. Is it

[122]New York: Doubleday, 1970, p. 362. See my *Who is Jesus of Nazareth?* p. 137.

any wonder that men were dazzled and blinded and cried out against him? Even his disciples cried out when he would not spare them the light. Is it any wonder that the priests realized that between this man and themselves, there was no choice, but that he or priestcraft should perish? Is it any wonder that the Roman soldiers, confronted and amazed by something soaring over their comprehension and threatening their discipline, should take refuge in wild laughter, crown him with thorns, robe him in purple and make a mock Caesar out of him? For to take him seriously was to enter a strange and alarming life, to abandon oneself to this life, to control instincts and impulses, to essay an incredible happiness .... Is it any wonder that to this day, this Galilean is too much for all our small hearts?

Such observations should at least serve as a warning of the danger of modernising Jesus, of forcing him into philosophical systems and categories of his own or any age. Although one cannot classify Jesus as a politician with a clear cut ideology and political programme yet his life and values had profound political consequences. Although he cannot be classified as a revolutionary, yet he was more radical than either the right or left. He was a question to all human concerns, priorities and preoccupations, above all, asking us whether we have the right concerns, priorities or preoccupations, not to mention our hidden agenda. Our task is to patiently work out the implications of our acceptance of Jesus for our time. The problem is that the New Testament has so little material "dealing directly with questions of social ethics and still less dealing with relations between peoples and nations."[123] Christian teaching has tended to echo that emphasis, being strongest in the area of the individual, weaker in that of the wider society and still weaker on the international plane.

[123]Berger Gerhardson, *The Ethos of the Bible,* (London: Darton, Longman & Todd, 1982), p. 16.

Martin Luther King

After much reflection, aided by the views of many scholars, we return as it were to the beginning. It is surprising how many recent scholars have concluded that John's gospel has got the correct approach to Jesus and politics. In that powerful scene Jesus decisively replies to Pilate's political question: "Are you the King of the Jews?" with the words "My Kingdom is not *of* this world!" But he does not say that his kingdom is not in this world. Here for John the distinctive sense of the term world is human society as it organises itself apart from God, as it is mobilized in defiance of the divine purpose. It corresponds roughly according to A.M. Hunter

> to the secularized world in which we are living today—the world of sex and violence, mods and rockers, nuclear bombs and morals without religion.[124]

It is the "brave new world" which T.S. Eliot once described as advancing progressively backwards because

> with its repudiation of traditional morality like the Ten Commandments and its scientific advance, of which the most horrific is the nuclear bomb, it has brought the mass of people not peace of mind but a certain nameless fear and foreboding and often a bleak sense of the futility and meaninglessness of life. Indeed where the secularizing process has gone furthest, the suicide rate has rocketed alarmingly, astrology has prospered, and mental illness increased almost beyond the power of medical science to cope with it.[125]

John has drawn out "the fascinating and fateful ambiguities, religious and political, inherent in the categories in which the

---

[124] *Preaching the New Testament*, (London: SCM, 1981).

[125] Ibid, pp. 131f.

person and work of Christ were composed.[126] The task of the Church is not to impose itself by force and violence but rather to sacrifice, to love, to forgive, to hope, to witness. The grain of wheat which dies is John's symbol (Jn 12:24). This does not mean that the political arena is abandoned. In John's presentation (Jn 18-19) Jesus himself is portrayed as witnessing for the truth before Pilate himself. That the reconciling Church should be distinguished from any narrowly based political party seems rather obvious, but to say that it has no business with the affairs of this world with the problems of peace and justice, with refugees, the hungry, the oppressed, with the 1,000 million who live in dreadful poverty or the 15,000 who die of starvation each day, seems a contradiction in terms and the direct opposite of what is said on so many pages of the Bible (e.g. Isa 1:15-17; 3:14-15). As the modern prophet, Martin Luther King once put it bluntly:

> Any religion that professes to be concerned about the souls of men and is not concerned about the slums that damn them, the economic conditions that strangle them, and the social conditions that cripple them, is a spiritually moribund religion awaiting burial.

But the Church, the guardian of mystery and the supernatural dimension must continually bear witness that politics alone can never solve the deeper issues and problems with which we are beset. As Jesus once said "Unless a person is born again he cannot see the kingdom of God" (Jn 3:9).

Kenneth Cragg

A very interesting reflection is often made by scholars such as Kenneth Cragg on the fundamental difference between Jesus' way and that of Mohammed, as each tried to respond to

---

[126]John A.T. Robinson, in Bammel and Moule, *Jesus and the Politics of His Day,* pp. 475/454.

similar situations.[127] Both preached a new way, gathered disciples and met with opposition from religious and political leaders and also with rejection and disaffection from their followers. Jesus, however, chose to continue in the same way. He accepted his rejection, failure and crucifixion. He put his faith in God despite his evident failure and rejected both the easy popularity of the wonder-worker and the quick success of armed force. Mohammed nearly took the same way of suffering. But he decided to fight for truth and to play the power-game seriously. He raised an army and marched to Mecca; the rest is history. Napoleon once observed that whereas Islam conquered half the world in ten years, Christianity took some three hundred years to establish itself. It was a messianic movement which like that of Jesus and the Baptist posed no military threat and had no hope of military victory, yet did provoke popular excitement and questioned the empire to its foundations. The important thing is that without an army the followers of Jesus, insignificant and powerless though they may have appeared, did eventually take over the mighty Roman Empire. But then there was the danger, the danger of becoming Constantine's friends.

C.E.B. Cranfield[128] who is convinced that every Christian has an inescapable obligation towards the state asks what are the reasons indicated in the NT for the Christian's political responsibility, what is its content and what guidance does the NT offer concerning the Spirit in which the Christian ought to fulfill his responsibility. He finds seven reasons:

1) Because a Christian is a beneficiary of the state (Mk 12:13-17).

2) For there is no power but of God (Rom 13:1; Jer 27:5f; Dan 2:21; Wis 6:3).

---

[127]K. Cragg, *The Call of the Minaret.* (New York: Oxford University Press, 1956); also *Jesus and the Muslim.* (London: Allen & Urwin, 1985).

[128]C.E.B. Cranfield, *The Bible and Christian Life,* pp. 50ff.

3) Authority is God's servant appointed to help Christians towards salvation and punish those who do evil (Rom 13:3f).

4) God wills the state as a means of promoting peace and quiet among people. Thus he desires that the state restrain the chaotic tendencies of people's self assertion, to maintain the conditions under which the gospel will be preached to all (1 Tim 2:1-7).

5) Subjection to the powers that be is part of that "reasonable service" or "understanding worship" which one should offer in gratitude to God for all he has done is, and will do in Jesus Christ (Rom 12:1ff).

6) Right service of the state is an integral part of our debt of love to our neighbours (Rom 12:9ff; 13:8-10).

7) All authority has been given to the exalted Christ (Mt 28:18; Rev 17:14; 19:16). As for the content of one's political responsibility the key work 'obey' (Rom 13:1; Tit 3:1; 1 Pet 2:13f) does not denote an uncritical, unquestioning obedience (Mk 12:17; Lk 13:32; Acts 5:29; 16:35ff).

Not only in a modern democracy but even in an authoritarian state a Christian owes the powers that be six things:

1) Respect—taking the government and its agents seriously as ministers of God, usually much more seriously than they take themselves. This does not mean flattery or that one has no claim to legal rights or that one cannot rebuke the authorities. (Rom 13:7; Acts 16:35; Mk 6:18; Lk 3:19).

2) Obedience so far as it does not involve disobeying God (Tit 3:1).

3) A serious and responsible disobedience, whenever obedience would involve disobeying God (Acts 4:19ff).

4) Payment of taxes (Mk 12:13-17; Rom 13:6f).

5) Prayer for those in authority (1 Tim 2:1ff).

6) Witness to Christ (Mk 13:9).

Further, in a democratic state a Christian has other obligations—

7) Responsible participation in parlimentary and municipal elections, in the fear of Christ and in love to one's neighbour.

8) A serious and sustained attempt to keep oneself as fully and realiably informed as possible concerning political issues.

9) Criticism of the government, its policies and its agents, in the light of the gospel and law of God.

10) An unceasing, untiring endeavour to support just and humane policies and to oppose those policies and particular decisions which are unjust or inhumane, by helping to build up an enlightened public opinion and in the various other ways (besides voting in election) which are constitutionally open to one.

11) The first and foremost service which the Christian owes the government and its agents is that he should himself be "swift to hear" the Word of God.

12) Readiness in certain circumstances and within certain limits, to join in military action at the command of the government. However, the N.T. nowhere gives a direct answer to the difficult question "Should a Christian refuse to take part in military service?" (Rom 13:4).

13) Readiness in certain extreme circumstances to engage in armed rebellion in order to overthrow a government that is intolerably unjust and to replace it. Again no direct guidance from the N.T. But the fact that our Lord was opposed to the Zealots does not mean that he would necessarily have discountenanced on principle, rebellion

in all circumstances. Cranfield insists that a Christian should in no circumstances whatsoever be willing to countenance the use of nuclear weapons.[129]

It might be best to leave the last to a poet because it needs a poet to express the depth of the foolishness that was Jesus' and his God's. The poet whom I select is the poet of the Irish Freedom movement, one who was willing to give his life for his dream, who dared to ask, 'O wise men, riddle me this: what

[129]Ibid., p. 53-54. Finally Cranfield draws three conclusions as to the N.T.'s guidance concerning the spirit in which a Christian ought to try to fulfil his political responsibility:

1) In all seriousness as an obligation from God, as a necessary part of his obedience to Jesus, of his debt of love to his neighbour, of his evangelistic responsibility, of that intelligent worship owed to God in gratitude.

2) In sobriety and realism because (of)

a) The eschatological teaching of the N.T. which makes clear the temporary nature of the state and so warns against all absolutizing of it.

b) The eschatological teaching of the N.T. which makes it clear that we cannot establish the kingdom of God by our political (or, for that matter, by our ecclesiastical) actions, and so forbids 'zealotism' with its inherent tendencies to fanaticism and ruthlessness.

c) The Christian must in the light of the N.T. reckon constantly with the fact that every member of the government, every official and every member of the electorate, in his own as in other countries is a sinner. He will be aware of the need at all times for safeguards designed to limit as much as possible the abuse of power, the need to scrutinize the claims, promises and high-sounding slogans of politicians.

d) A realisation that there are limits to what can be achieved in the sphere of politics and that therefore limited goals are not to be despised.

e) A recognition that the purpose of civil government and of the state in God's intention is a purpose of mercy towards all men for whom Christ died(1 Tim 2:1ff; Rom 14:15; 1 Cor 8:11; Mt 25:40ff).

3) In confidence of hope because:

a) God is in control over the state and civil authority. E.g. Pontius Pilate, unworthy and unwilling servant though he was, nevertheless God's perfect will for the redemption of mankind was accomplished through him.

b) Political affairs no less than the life of the Church are within the domain of Christ (Rev 1:5; Mt 28:18).

c) The end toward which history moves is the coming in glory of Jesus Christ, the decisive and unambiguous establishment of God's new order, his kingdom (Rev 11:15; 21:24).

if the dream come true?' 'since the wise men have not spoken, I
speak,' said Pearse, 'that am only a fool.'[130]

'A fool that hath loved his folly.
Yea, more than the wise men their books or their counting
houses, or their quiet homes,
Or their fame in men's mouths;
A fool that in all his days hath done never a prudent thing,
Never hath counted the cost nor recked if another reaped
The fruit of his mighty sowing, content to scatter the seed;
A fool that is unrepentant, and that soon at the end of all
Shall laugh in his lonely heart as the ripe ears fall to the
reaping hooks
And the poor are filled that were empty
Tho' he go hungry.

I have squandered the splendid years that the Lord God
gave to my youth
In attempting impossible things, deeming them alone worth
the toil.
Was it folly or grace? Not men shall judge me, but God.
I have squandered the splendid years:
Lord, if I had the years I would squander them over again,
Aye, fling them from me!
For this I have heard in my heart, that a man shall scatter,
not hoard.
Shall do the deed of to-day, nor take thought of to-morrow's
teen,
Shall not bargain nor huxter with God; or was it a jest of
Christ's
And is this my sin before men, to have taken him at his
word?'

[130]P. Pearse, *Plays, Stories, Poems.* (Dublin: Phoenix Pub. Co., 1917; rep.
1980).

Bibliography

E. Bammel & C.F.D. Moule (Ed.), *Jesus & the Politics of His Day* (Cambridge: University Press, 1984).

Leonard Boff, *Jesus Christ Liberator* (London: S.P.C.K., 1980).

Robert McAfee Brown, *Unexpected News* (Philadelphia: Westminster Press, 1984).

Richard J. Cassidy, *Jesus, Politics and Society* (New York: Orbis, 1980).

Michael Clevenot, *Materialist Approaches to the Bible* (New York: Orbis, 1985).

C.E.B. Cranfield, *The Bible & Christian Life* (Edinburgh: T & T Clark, 1985).

James D.G. Dunn, *The Evidence for Jesus* (London: S.C.M., 1985).

Joseph A. Fitzmyer, S.J., *A Christological Catechism* (New York: Paulist, 1982).

J. Massyngbaerde Ford, *My Enemy is my Guest* (New York: Orbis, 1984).

Sean Freyne, *Galilee from Alexander the Great to Hadrian* (Notre Dame: University Press, 1980).

John H. Hayes, *Son of God to Superstar* (Nashville: Abingdon, 1976).

M. Hengel, *Was Jesus a Revolutionary?* (Philadelphia: Fortress Press, 1971).

Sean P. Kealy, C.S.Sp., *Who is Jesus of Nazareth?* (New Jersey: Dimension Books, 1978).

H.M. Kiutert, *Everything is Politics but Politics is not Everything* (London: S.C.M., 1986).

Gerhard Lohfink, *Jesus & Community* (New York: Paulist, 1984).

Gerald O'Collins, *Interpreting Jesus* (Ramsey: Paulist, 1983).

Ellis Rivkin, *What Crucified Jesus?* (Nashville: Abingdon, 1984).

E.P. Sanders, *Jesus & Judaism* (London: S.C.M., 1984).

William M. Thompson, *The Jesus Debate,* (New York: Paulist Press, 1985).

John Ziesler, *The Jesus Question,* (London: Lutterworth, 1980).

Indices

Author Index

Subject Index

Scripture Index
OLD TESTAMENT

NEW TESTAMENT